"Dr. Gina is one of the only mental health experts willing to stand against her own profession when it's wrong. Her analysis of the interplay between politics and psychology is unparalleled in media today. Read her book, and understand how to see through the politics, into a deeper ability to discern the truths of our time."

—Katrina Pierson, Senior Advisor, Donald J. Trump Campaign 2020, and 2016 Spokeswoman for Donald J. Trump for President

"*Mad Politics* is the book my generation needs to read, because there is so much noise out there, and we need the tools to discern the truth out there in this crazy world! Dr. Loudon speaks right to parents and young people like me when she lays out her vision for the best tomorrow possible, and how we can get there together. Your family and you will laugh when you read her anecdotes about parenting her own children in this mixed-up world, but you will be closer when you read her steps to staying sane together, and making your mark on the future of this great country. Dr. Loudon has given us a road map and the tools to navigate our way through the mire. *Mad Politics* is a book for all ages and a must-read for millennials who want to make a difference in the world. As a young activist, I can't recommend *Mad Politics* enough."

—Kyle Kashuv, student at Marjory Stoneman Douglas High School and director of high school outreach, Turning Point USA

r. Gina Loudon is a force of nature. She has the compassion of a ther of five, the depth of a credentialed psychoanalyst, the savvy of teran broadcaster, the burning passion of a liberty lover, and the ts of a genuine Trump political insider. In *Mad Politics*, Dr. Gina down and explains the psychosis of the left, provides tools for anding their misguided, absolutist strategies against President nd charts a course for improving American culture in time for en's children to live in liberty once again. President Trump is o have such a great defender in Dr. Gina Loudon, and the movement is very, very fortunate to have her on our side!"

rrano, Strategic Communications Consultant and a visor to the 2020 Trump Campaign

PRAISE FOR MAD POLITICS

"This book outlines exactly what the American people need to know. President Donald J. Trump is the change agent that Washington, D.C., has needed for the last thirty years. Dr. Loudon has witnessed firsthand the promises made and promises kept by President Trump."

   —Corey R. Lewandowski, Campaign Manager, Donald J. Trump
      for President 2016

"In a world gone crazy, Dr. Gina Loudon's levelheaded analysis is a breath of fresh air. Resolute in her manner, she ardently defends those to whom she is loyal day after day. In her presence, one is immediately aware of her kindness and compassion, but cannot overlook her wit and savvy. I am lucky to call her a friend and I proudly declare her a patriot."

   —Lara Trump, Trump 2020 Senior Campaign Advisor

"As the Campaign Manager for President Trump, I see the rava brought about on our nation by those who attempt to divide dehumanize every day. Thank God that Dr. Gina took her logical lens and applied it to all of the left's craziness, so th approach 2020 with more sanity, and a better understa we got to this amazing moment in history! *Mad Politi* the insanity and nails it for just what it is—a dis calls on us to have the same mental clarity and s dent, Donald J. Trump. With him at the helm and make it the very best in history, togethe that journey, and start by reading her bo through the insanity on the left, and s best, ever, when we re-elect Donald

   —Brad Parscale, Campaign M

"Dr. Gina has been a pro-Tr spent many hours on air book is a must read for a American politics."

   —Eric Bolling, author of *Wake*

"Dr. Gina's enviable resume—psychology expert, pundit, and wife of a successful politician—creates the ideal combination of experience and critical mind to analyze the craziness in our current political climate and what it does to different groups. This book is the perfect vaccine."

—Dr. Dathan Paterno, Licensed Clinical Psychologist

"Tribalism and group think are being normalized as vitriol has become synonymous with communication. With elected officials modeling toxic behavior and refusing to engage beyond party affiliation, voters' ability to understand the interconnected roots of issues, learn nuances, and equip themselves with the right tools necessary to make thoughtful, personal decisions is being stymied at the very source. If anyone can help guide us all back to that point of congenial discourse and thoughtful engagement, it's Dr. Gina!"

—Emily Compagno, Attorney and legal analyst

"Dr. Loudon understands the MAGA movement and the great Americans who elected this president!"

—Kayleigh McEnany, GOP Spokeswoman

"Dr. Gina is a tremendous person, who is equally dedicated to her faith, family, and country. Hersteadfast support for our president and vice president is making America great. Since firstvoicing her support for President Trump, she has articulately and clearly represented theforgotten men and women who are forgotten no more. She is an invaluable friend to us here atthe Trump Campaign."

—John Pence, Senior Advisor to the Trump Campaign

"Dr. Gina cuts through the confusion that makes us feel cynical and hopeless in the world of politics today. If it all seems too crazy at times, grab a copy of this book to help make sense of it all, and find your way in this confusing world of politics. A must-read for those participating in all levels of politics!"

—Morgan Ortagus, Co-founder of GO Advisory, National Co-Chair of Maverick PAC

MAD POLITICS

MAD POLITICS

Keeping Your Sanity in a World Gone Crazy

DR. GINA LOUDON

FOREWORD BY SEAN HANNITY

REGNERY
PUBLISHING
A Division of Salem Media Group

Regnery® is a registered trademark of Salem Communications Holding Corporation

Cataloging-in-Publication data on file with the Library of Congress

ISBN 978-1-62157-803-1
ebook ISBN 978-1-62157-840-6

Published in the United States by
Regnery Publishing
A Division of Salem Media Group
300 New Jersey Ave NW
Washington, DC 20001
www.Regnery.com

Manufactured in the United States of America

10 9 8 7 6 5 4 3 2

Dedicated to the reasons I fight…

*To the glory of God alone, who saw fit to let us live in the
best country, at the best moment in history! We really have it all.
God Bless America, and America, Bless GOD!*

*For my children, Lyda Lindsey, Lily Love, John William Jr. "Jack,"
Samuel Christian, and Robert Brewster III "Bo," along with my
husband, John, and my friends who have the courage to fight.*

*And to our President who stands courageously every day
that America might continue to be the hope for freedom for
the whole world! Thank you, Donald J. Trump!*

Contents

PART THREE: THE CURE FOR CRAZY

FOREWORD BY SEAN HANNITY

They think you're crazy. The other side seriously thinks *you* are the crazy one!

But let's examine their premise for a moment.

Why do they think *you* are the crazy one? You don't agree with them. That's why. It's seriously that simple.

They ignore truth and common sense, they refuse to even come on my show and debate me, they unfollow and block you for dissent on social media, and they lack critical thinking skills that are integral to rational decision making. They are angry! And no wonder, because they are the ones who make no sense.

The brainwashing goes deep with the new generation of "leftist lemmings," as Dr. Loudon calls them in her book, *Mad Politics*. They are often raised like snowflakes. They have never taken a Western Civilization course, so they don't understand the basis of what works and what doesn't. They graduate their safe space high school to live in their mother's basement with dreams of Twitter trolls dancing in their heads. They enter a six-year, tax-funded, university indoctrination program like feminist studies, hoping (not praying, because they don't do that) that

George Soros will hire them to astroturf his next staged protest against truth. If they do get to become part of the elite, even a little part, they will do anything to please those on high. It's the definition of crazy.

In *Mad Politics: Keeping Your Sanity in a World Gone Crazy*, Dr. Loudon lays out your counter case to their accusation that you are the crazy one. A twice pedigreed master's student with a PhD, she grabs on to her roots in the South and Midwest and speaks the plain truth in a common sense way for the common sense reader who really wants to battle the lies of the left.

Narcissistic politicians, schizophrenic headlines, and obsessive witch hunts abound. Western civilization and fundamental truths are edited or deleted, and lemming/snowflake mentality is the rule in the press, our schools, and even our workplaces today.

Mad Politics is the remarkable case for sanity where there is only crazy, for "adulting" where the other side acts like children, for bravery in the face of snowflake safe spaces, and for common sense where there is hysteria. In a world that seems crazy, Dr. Loudon spells out the ways that liberal logic is indeed the bud of insanity, and how conservatives stand poised to restore sanity based on truth, conviction, reason, and research.

She has done all the footwork for you to respond to even the harshest of assaults on your faith, your family, and your freedom. Her step-by-step roadmap to restoring America's sanity will engage you, encourage you, and empower you in ways you never thought possible, and leave you with a strong sense of direction in a confusing culture.

Dr. Loudon weaves in her personal experience in academia and the green rooms of TV and radio networks across the country, where she has met "the crazy" face to face, battled it, and become the authority on how to restore sanity, no matter how crazy the crazy might seem.

She is one of the few I have trusted with my microphone, and a frequent guest on my shows, because I trust her down-to-earth, honest, psychological analysis on the political issues that come at us like a firehose today!

This book is a breath of fresh air in the smog of liberal hypocrisy that has polluted our lives for far too long. Dr. Loudon's *Mad Politics* will humor you, entertain you, encourage you, and inspire you to be part of the return to sanity in the political arena.

From Constitutional soundness to Biblical doctrine, Gina paints a road map of restoration, and you get to join me in the adventure!

Let not your heart be troubled, my friends! Less expensive than a therapy session that probably wouldn't help you anyway, read this account of a skilled psychology expert, a devoted mom, and a fierce and fearless patriot who has a strategy to restore the truth that is salve for your soul and wings for your spirit, as we boldly restore America's sanity together!

PART ONE

THE GOOD KIND
OF CRAZY

CHAPTER 1

DRIVING HIS OPPONENTS MAD

Trump's Greatest Accomplishment

"All the world is mad, but thee and me, and even thou art a little crazy."

—Adapted from Robert Owen

Donald J. Trump descended the escalator into the lobby of Trump Tower in New York City on June 16, 2015, and drove the media crazy with these words:

> When Mexico sends its people, they're not sending their best. They're not sending you. They're not sending you. They're sending people that have lots of problems, and they're bringing those problems with us. They're bringing drugs. They're bringing crime. They're rapists. And some, I assume, are good people.[1]

Or did he say, "They're bringing crime, *their* rapists, and some, I assume, are good people"?

The media immediately whipped themselves into a frenzy, deciding that if Donald Trump were going to run as a Republican, he *must* be a racist.

From that moment, every week, sometimes multiple times per week, there has been a media meltdown.

The media went mad. The media made people mad. Trump made the media mad. Candidate Trump used his mad skills to drive the media mad. The media accused Trump supporters of being mad, and they were! Mad at media, mad at the injustice, mad at the subversion of our Constitution, mad at the mounting threats against America that President Obama left unanswered. And mad that Hillary Clinton felt entitled to the presidency despite the crime and corruption of the Clinton cartel.

Yes, the electorate was mad, but not crazy. In fact, they may have been saner in their anger than ever before, with a clear path to victory like never before, and a candidate with mad skills like never before.

If I have been asked once in my television commentary, I have been asked a hundred times: Is President Trump crazy?

Yes, I answer, he is. He is crazy like a fox, and it's driving them all crazy!

It seems that winning is simply in this president's DNA, and it drives the left insane. They perfectly fit the proverbial definition of insanity: doing the same thing over and over and expecting a different result. That is what the media does every day. Not the president, though.

He gets up every day and changes his tactics just enough to provoke another hissy fit, more ferocious than the day before. His base applauds, and I have to admit, I laugh out loud almost every day at his ability to make his detractors crazy.

After all they did to sabotage this man and his family, the best the media could hope for when he won the election was a do-nothing presidency. They could bully the Democrats into being the obstructionists they always said they weren't so the president couldn't accomplish anything.

But much as he finesses the media into their own madness, the president drove the Democrats into that same spiral by checking off more than eighty agenda items in his first year alone and repealing eleven Obama legacy items, with no help from them.

Winners and losers

The *Washington Examiner* cataloged some of Trump's biggest accomplishments on the first anniversary of his presidency.[2]

He revived the economy and restored jobs with his landmark tax reform, which also repealed the Obamacare mandate, and GDP growth was well on its way to 4 percent.

1.7 million Americans had new jobs, and unemployment had dropped to 4.1 percent.

The stock market skyrocketed, boosting consumer confidence to a seventeen-year high. And for all the left's whining about Trump's hating women, he initiated some $500 million in new SBA loans for women-owned businesses.

But he didn't stop there.

American business had been strangled by job-killing regulations imposed by an Obama administration with delusions of omnicompetence. President Trump ordered that two regulations be eliminated for each new one imposed. But he beat himself at his own game, killing about sixteen regulations for *every* new one and saving business about $8.1 billion.

Media heads spun when he withdrew from Obama's Paris Climate Accord and ended other environmentalist measures choking coal and other business.

He withdrew from the anti-American Trans-Pacific Partnership and tightened up enforcement of U.S. trade laws. He ended Obama's deal with the corrupt Cuban regime.

He unleashed American energy and oil when he opened 77 million acres for drilling in the Gulf of Mexico. He approved construction of the Keystone XL pipeline and ended the forty-year-old ban on drilling in the Arctic National Wildlife Refuge in Alaska.

One of his key campaign promises to Angel Moms, legal immigrants, and American citizens in general was to solve America's dangerous and out-of-control illegal immigration problem. He ended Obama's catch-and-release program and cracked down on so-called sanctuary cities. He added more than a hundred new immigration judges and removed almost 40 percent more criminal gang members than were removed in the year before his election. Homeland Security rounded up almost eight hundred MS-13 members, 83 percent more than the year before.

Another key issue for Trump's base was activist judges. Trump nominated more than seventy-three federal judges and topped it off with the nomination of Neil Gorsuch to the Supreme Court. This especially pleased his religious base, who had been unfairly victimized again and again when Obama and the ACLU weaponized the judicial branch of government. But the president didn't stop there.

Living near Palm Beach, Florida, I know a lot of people who know the president and who knew him well before he was president. I myself have experienced his loyalty to those who have been good to him, but that loyalty was never more beautifully on display than when he defanged the Johnson Amendment, which was used to bully pastors who share a Gospel perspective on public affairs, and when he recognized Jerusalem as the rightful capital of Israel by moving our embassy there.

Taking that stand with Israel was a promise that even Trump's most enthusiastic religious supporters might have doubted he could keep, but he did, and he did it in the first year of his presidency. It was a clear message to his base that he would keep his promises, regardless of the mockery of the left, who were losing their minds over his ability to win despite them.

One of the issues near to my heart wasn't on the elites' radar, but Trump heard about it from Main Street America, who asked for his help. That is why I was so honored when I was asked to speak on the president's Facebook page about the opioid crisis and his commitment to solve it.

He began his war on opioids by declaring the problem a nationwide public health emergency and allotting $500 million to fight this national crisis. He addressed the illegal sales of opioids from China on his trip there late in 2017. Hundreds of arrests were made, and 456 tons of drugs were seized in one day by the Drug Enforcement Administration.

While most Republicans avoid the abortion issue for politically pragmatic reasons, this president made defending life a centerpiece of his first year. In his first week in office, he reinstated and even expanded the "Mexico City policy," which blocked millions of dollars in foreign aid that would have paid to kill babies overseas.

He didn't forget his promises to veterans, either. He restored accountability to the Department of Veterans Affairs with the Veterans Accountability and Whistleblower Protection Act, allocated $2.1 billion for the Veterans Choice Program, and set up a hotline to report abuse. He reduced wait times and improved the quality of care at VA health centers.

Perhaps his most herculean but unheralded accomplishment was his victory over ISIS. Many haven't noticed that ISIS attacks, a common occurrence under Obama, are virtually a thing of the past. No more would Americans go to sleep under the threat of Islamic terrorist attacks, and no more would they wake up to news of yet another Islamic terrorist act. Such atrocities became fewer and farther apart, and the media were silent.

President Trump funded and rebuilt the military while auditing the Pentagon to look for wasteful expenditures. He restored the National Space Council, enabling new space war strategies to combat our enemies with technology they don't have. He repudiated the United Nations' New York Declaration for Refugees and Migrants, an affront to U.S. sovereignty, and imposed a travel ban on nations that lack terror security, using Obama's own list of the most dangerous countries.

Sometimes his foreign policy was as amusing to his base as it was maddening to his detractors. North Korea decided to test this president immediately to see if he was as feckless as his predecessor. President Trump sent the media and the Swamp into a tizzy when he responded on Twitter, "I told Rex Tillerson, our wonderful Secretary of State, that he is wasting his time trying to negotiate with Little Rocket Man"—his pet name for the dictator Kim Jong-un. While the left in their fury called for the president's impeachment, President Moon Jae-in of South Korea credited him with bringing the North to the negotiation table.

Bringing a brutal dictator to the negotiating table with a tweet was unheard of, to say the least. President Trump proved again that his way of leading was not that of the dour old media and that he could get the job done while they lost their minds about his tactics. It is estimated that in his first year, he completed one monumental accomplishment every thirty-six hours. I argued on Twitter that his mental stability and stamina far surpassed his attackers, because few could be so productive while their families, friends, livelihoods, and very existence were constantly under threat. But he did. And it drove them mad.

They will never appreciate him. They can't. They are too invested in their cushy lifestyles, their friendships on Capitol Hill, their friendships with Coastal elites who own most of the nation's wealth, and playing in the Swamp with them. There is no way they will admit they've been wrong. They have what some have called "Trump Derangement Syndrome." There is no known cure.

Losing can be maddening. If the talk show host Michael Savage is right, and liberalism is indeed a mental disorder, then the media's tendency to lose its mind in reaction to Trump is less puzzling.

I'm afraid the only advice I have for these poor unhinged folks is to join the winning side. Seriously! Buck up, admit you've been wrong (we have all been there), then come on in—the water's fine! And the winning is so much *fun*!

More winning on the horizon

The lamestream media and the establishment elites have convinced themselves that the 2016 election was a fluke, a minor setback. They will get back on the road to big government as soon as they can get rid of Trump in 2020, or impeach him some how, some way.

The elites knew the Russians didn't rig the election, and they knew that there was no collusion between the Trump campaign and Vladimir Putin.

The elites believed the commoners just needed an outlet. They needed to relieve a little pressure. They were right about that, but they were wrong in thinking that American voters were going to revert to submission and apathy.

The second wave of the citizen uprising is coming. And there is nothing the establishment can do about it unless they can figure out a way to derail a freight-train economy that has a full head of steam.

The first wave of the citizen uprising was a reaction to Obama's fundamental transformation of America.

President Trump's election wasn't the beginning of this uprising, though. Democrats have been losing elections for years. They are steadily losing seats, state legislatures and governorships nationwide.

And the biggest election they lost was the 2016 presidential election, and it won't be the last.

This first wave of the citizen uprising swept the big-government globalists out of power. The second wave is now beginning, and will crest in the next few years as the success of free-market capitalism is realized once again in America and the world.

As people get to keep more of their money, as corporations give bonuses and pay raises to employees, as companies move their operations back to the United States, and as America's economy grows again, a second wave of support for the America First agenda will sweep more Trump-allied Republicans into elected office.

Confounding the experts

On Christmas Day 2017, I briefly tuned in to cable news. It was a pretty light news day, and they ran a clip of Trump declaring "When I'm president, we're going to say 'Merry Christmas' in America again!" A mocking journalist sniffed, "The war on Christmas has been way overblown, and no one was ever not allowed to say 'Merry Christmas' in America."

This highly educated journalist missed the entire point of the president's comments. The president wasn't just talking about saying the words "Merry Christmas." Every Trump supporter outside of the D.C. bubble understood exactly what the president meant when he said that.

The president meant that he would end the war on *Christianity*. He meant that we would no longer be forced to pay for other people's abortions, that nuns wouldn't be forced to provide contraceptives, that bakers wouldn't be forced to make cakes that defied their religious values, that schoolchildren wouldn't be forced into unisex bathrooms and locker rooms.

The president didn't have to say all of that. All he had to say was. "We are going to say 'Merry Christmas' in America again." We all understood that he was talking about an end to Obama's war on religion.

The same with the wall.

When the president said, "We are going to build a great wall," we all understood that it was more than just a wall. It meant guarding our border, more ICE agents, ending chain migration, cracking down on visa overstays, mandatory e-verification—in other words, what every sovereign country does to maintain its sovereign borders.

Everyone outside the coastal elites knew what Donald Trump meant.

When candidate Trump called for building the wall, the so-called experts laughed at his simplistic solution. And we all laughed at the simplistic experts. Every voter in middle America knew that Trump was talking about more than just a wall. "The wall" was an image of a safer America. The experts said he didn't understand, yet he understood better than any of them.

He didn't have to explain, because he was speaking for us.

The disruptor's disrupter

I am often asked to name President Trump's greatest accomplishment.

His Supreme Court appointments will, I pray, be a legacy for decades to come. His recognition of Jerusalem as the capital of Israel will secure him a place in the history books. His policy of cutting taxes and regulations has given the economy new life like we haven't seen for decades.

But I believe President Trump's greatest accomplishment isn't something that will be a chapter in a history book. The president's greatest accomplishment has been *driving the left mad*.

In the past, Republicans have ignored attacks from the left, hoping they would stop, or conceded ground, hoping the left would love them. And every time they did this, we watched in disgust as those we elected to stand for us cowered like spineless pink cocktail shrimp.

Two things are certain in American politics. First, the left will never stop attacking. Second, the left will never love us, no matter how quickly and completely we capitulate.

President Trump is pursuing a strategy that *no* Republican president has pursued before: He is constantly on the offensive. President George W. Bush never responded to the left's attacks. He was "presidential," but by the end of his presidency, the caricature of Bush as a war-mongering idiot was ingrained in the minds of Americans. By acting "presidential," he had allowed the left to brand him.

President Trump understands branding as well as the left does. If you repeat something enough, it will stick in the minds of those who hear it. If a person hears a lie over and over, he eventually starts to believe it. So repeat after me:

Republicans are bigots.

Republicans are sexist.

Republicans hate poor people.

Republicans don't care about children.

Republicans want old people to die.

Republicans want to destroy the environment.

Republicans want to take away your health care.

President Trump took the left's own trick and used it on them. He repeated the moniker "Crooked Hillary" ten thousand times on the campaign trail. And by the end of the campaign, every voter knew Hillary Clinton was corrupt.

If GOP leaders had been doing that for the past two decades, Bill and Hillary might have slithered back into their hole a long time ago. Imagine what might have been different! No pay-to-play scheme in the State Department, funneling cash from foreign governments to the Clinton Foundation. No Uranium One deal, handing over a large portion of

America's uranium to the Russians. No top-secret information hacked from Hillary's unsecure email server. And who knows what other evils we would have avoided if the Bonnie and Clyde of American politics had been as far from power as they should have been?

But instead of branding the Clintons as corrupt, GOP leaders decided to leave them alone. It wasn't "presidential" for President Bush to call out the corruption of the Clinton administration. The GOP leaders might not get invited to the right Georgetown cocktail parties anymore if they told the truth about the Clintons.

Lives were lost and our nation's secrets were stolen because the Clintons faced no consequences for their corruption. Republican leaders couldn't even be pressured to say something unkind about the corrupt Clintons for fear of being shunned by the establishment.

President Trump finally called the Clintons out for their corruption, and today Bill and Hillary are shunned by those who used to be their besties. President Trump, with his branding genius, has finally removed the Clinton crime family from politics.

Over the years, the spinelessness of the GOP leadership was maddening to watch. We always wondered what they were so afraid of. We still do. That same spinelessness keeps us from attaining what we could if the GOP would stand firm instead of running scared at every opportunity.

So when the left describes Trump voters as "mad," they're right. We're mad at those who won't stand up.

It's hard to believe today, but many of us had hopes for Obama once upon a time. We hoped his election would end the racism and division in our country and bring about the unity that was informally promised "if we would ever elect a black president." We did that. We weren't demanding a recount or an impeachment. We weren't trying to overturn an election. We were trying to support our president as much as we could.

When he bowed to foreign rulers, bashed America, mocked our Constitution, attacked our country's moral foundation, danced on the graves of our founders and war heroes, strangled our economy, broke our health care system, killed our unborn babies, destroyed our jobs, colluded with our enemies, sowed division, and insulted our intelligence, we couldn't support him. But it wasn't because he was a Democrat. It was because he was dangerous.

As much as we came to despise his policies, we had initially hoped and prayed for his success. We were ready to put partisanship aside and work with him where we could agree. But all that good will collided with an iron law of American politics: The left cannot win on the issues, so they have to disrupt, divide, and divert—and import voters from foreign countries.

That's where we come to the seemingly crazy Democrat immigration policy.

People often ask me why we can't just come to some sort of agreement with the Democrats on immigration reform. The answer is that they can't negotiate with us, or they won't win elections.

It may seem totally insane for the left to take such a lax stance on illegal immigration. Why would anyone support the dangerous policy of open borders and unfettered illegal immigration? Why would the left insist on bringing refugees from terror-prone countries where the left's own favorite causes—like the rights of women and minorities—are low priorities? Because there are not enough Americans who will vote for them. Their only hope is to import non-Americans and give them enough free stuff to win their votes.

That's also why the left opposes merit-based immigration, which favors those more likely to contribute to and benefit from our capitalist economy. A skilled and ambitious young programmer who is unlikely to depend on government assistance is not the kind of guaranteed Democratic voter the left favors.

The safety of the American people does not drive Democratic immigration policy. Power is their number-one priority. Anything that gets in the way of that is to be damned.

Even illegal immigrants from Latin countries begin to align with important GOP policies after they get here. This is another problem for Democrats. Latinos are largely religious and family-oriented, and protecting religion and family are planks in the Republican platform. The Democrats, on the other hand, removed God from their platform, and they want to redefine not only family, but male and female. Those values don't fly with Latinos, so Democrats need to persuade the newcomers that conservatives hate them. Racial division is all they have to offer.

The same is true for immigrants from the former Eastern Bloc countries. They understand freedom because they have lived without it. So, after a couple of years in America, even when the left offers them welfare and socialist health care, they see through it. They know that Democrats want big government, and that big government means power over people. They learn about the patriots who died to preserve freedom in America as the left tries to convince them that freedom is free.

People who have lived under tyranny are unlikely to trade their freedom for what the Democrats are offering. They see the left trying to take guns, and they know what happens when the guns are gone. They see the left kneeling during the national anthem, and they remember the cost of freedom. Immigrants from the former Eastern Bloc therefore gravitate toward political conservatism.

Asian culture emphasizes math, science, and industry. They know fake science when they see it, and they tend to resent it when the left turns "renewable energy" into a corporate welfare program for wealthy opportunists or tries to sacrifice entire industries on the altar of global warming. Asians are famously hard workers, and they tend to take offense at the left's redistribution of the fruits of their labor. Therefore, once they are here, they trend conservative too.

If you listened to the media, you would think that armies of angry white men goose-stepped to the polls in 2016 to elect Trump after he stirred their racist passions. Yet the numbers show that not to be true. President Trump carried the white vote by the same margin as Mitt Romney did in 2012, but he outperformed Romney, to the confusion of the experts, among black and Hispanic voters.

Black and Hispanic voters, in fact, put Trump over the top in his race against Hillary Clinton. Expect his support among them to grow in

2020, as black home ownership soars to all-time highs, while black, Latino, and female unemployment have reached record lows, and jobs abound. This will change so much for black communities in America and may prove once and for all that black Americans have a real political home in the GOP, where family, faith, and freedom are valued. Hispanic immigrants will love the safe neighborhoods they can enjoy when immigrant gangs stop terrorizing their streets and stealing their children. And the chaos in cities that have been controlled by Democrats for decades will expose the lie that somehow Democrats "care more" about black families. The record speaks for itself.

Perhaps Muslims are the least culturally aligned with conservatives because Western culture is so different from Middle Eastern culture. I will address that more in a later chapter, but the chasm between Muslims and Western culture explains why the left is so tolerant of Islamic terror. Their political survival may rely on massive Islamic immigration.

Voters weren't fooled by the media's insistence that Donald Trump is racist. When candidate Trump talked about putting America first, we all understood that he was talking about all Americans regardless of their skin color.

He said he wanted to be president "of all Americans." He asked minorities whose communities and families have been ravaged by leftist policies and whose children lie dead in the street what they really had to lose in voting for him. They continue to migrate toward this movement, this ideal, of true tolerance, real reform, free faith, and expansive freedom.

President Trump preached economic nationalism, meaning that if you're an American citizen, then you will be better off with him regardless your race. That message spoke to blue-collar Democrats in traditionally blue states, and it spoke to enough minority voters across the country that Donald Trump was elected the forty-fifth president of the United States.

CHAPTER 2

MAD
SKILLS

How Trump Used Social Media
to Mobilize a Revolution

*"I use social media not because I like to, but because it
is the only way to fight a VERY dishonest and unfair
'press,' now often referred to as Fake News Media. Phony
and non-existent 'sources' are being used more often than
ever. Many stories & reports a pure fiction!"*
  —Donald J. Trump, Twitter, December 20, 2017

*"Those who make peaceful revolution impossible make
violent revolution inevitable."*
  —John F. Kennedy

R evolution is never bloodless. It's almost unbearable to consider the
sacrifices our Founders made to give us our great America.

There is one person I look to whenever I have a question about history because of the incomparable depth and breadth of his knowledge.

When my husband was running for office in Missouri in the 1990s, I went to a bookstore to find a book to help him brush up on historic speeches. There are few places I would rather shop than a bookstore, and on this day, I was delighted to find *America's God and Country* by Bill Federer.

That evening we went to a political social, where I shared my excitement about finding this wonderfully comprehensive yet concise book with a circle of people gathered around me. When I mentioned the title, a man in the group said quietly, "That's my book."

I responded with that awkward smile reserved for those moments where you have no idea what someone just said even though you heard him perfectly. A woman who would become a mentor to me, Lois Linton, said, "How incredible that you bought his book and met him tonight!"

In disbelief, I glanced back at the man. "Wait, what is your name?" I asked.

"Well, the book calls me William, but I you can call me Bill. Bill Federer. Nice to meet you! Did you say your husband was running for office?"

"No, wait," I insisted, "I am still confused. You're telling me that you are the author of the book I randomly purchased today, and was so excited about that I brought it up at this party, and you are the author standing right here in front of me? Am I in some reality show?"

He laughed politely. It *was* his book, a remarkable book that I still keep on my special shelf of favorites. And Bill Federer has not just become a guide and friend to my husband and me over the years – he has also become America's Favorite Historian.

When I began to consider writing a book about how this president and his "Make America Great Again" movement had pulled off a bloodless revolution, I wrote to Bill asking for his historical perspective. I'm delighted to share with some excerpts from his response regarding the courage nearing pure madness of what our Founding Fathers gave us:

America's Independence
William J. Federer[1]

Thirty-eight-year-old King George III ruled the largest empire that earth had ever seen.

In the Declaration of Independence, approved July 4, 1776, Americans listed the reasons that "impelled them to the separation" from that king and empire:

He has made judges dependent on his will alone…

He has erected a multitude of new offices, and sent hither swarms of officers to harass our people and eat out their substance.

He has kept among us, in times of peace, standing armies...

He has combined with others to subject us to a jurisdiction foreign to our constitution, and unacknowledged by our law; giving his assent to their acts of pretended legislation:

For quartering large bodies of armed troops among us...

For imposing taxes on us without our consent...

For depriving us, in many cases, of the benefits of trial by jury...

For...altering fundamentally the forms of our governments...

He has plundered our seas, ravaged our coasts, burnt our towns, and destroyed the lives of our people.

He is, at this time, transporting large armies of foreign mercenaries to complete the works of death, desolation, and tyranny, already begun with circumstances of cruelty and perfidy, scarcely paralleled in the most barbarous ages, and totally unworthy the head of a civilized nation...

He has excited domestic insurrections amongst us, and has endeavored to bring on the inhabitants of our frontiers, the merciless Indian savages, whose known rule of warfare, is an undistinguished destruction of all ages, sexes and conditions...

Thirty-three-year-old Thomas Jefferson's original draft of the Declaration contained a condemnation of slavery:

He has waged cruel war against human nature itself, violating its most sacred rights of life and liberty in the persons of a distant people who never offended him, captivating and carrying them into slavery in another hemisphere, or to incur miserable death, in their transportation thither.

A few delegates objected, and since time was running short (the British were invading New York) and the Declaration needed to pass unanimously, the condemnation of slavery was unfortunately omitted.

John Hancock, the thirty-nine-year-old president of the Continental Congress, signed the Declaration first, reportedly saying, "The price on my head has just doubled."

Next to sign was the secretary, Charles Thomson, age forty-seven.

Seventy-year-old Benjamin Franklin cautioned his comrades, "We must hang together or most assuredly we shall hang separately."

The Declaration referred to God:

... the laws of nature and of *nature's God*... all men are created equal, that they are endowed by their *Creator* with certain unalienable rights... Appealing to the *Supreme Judge of the world* for the rectitude of our intentions... And for the support of this Declaration, with a firm reliance on the protection of *Divine Providence*, we mutually pledge to each other our lives, our fortunes, and our sacred honor.

This was revolutionary in the age of the "divine right of kings," when it was believed that the Creator gives rights to the king, who dispenses them at his discretion to his subjects. The American Declaration by passes the king, declaring that the Creator gives rights directly to "all men."

Many of the fifty-six signers sacrificed their prosperity for their posterity: eleven suffered the destruction of their homes, five were hunted and captured, seventeen served in the military, and nine died during the war.

Twenty-seven-year-old George Walton was wounded and captured at the battle of Savannah.

Edward Rutledge, age twenty-seven, Thomas Heyward Jr., age thirty, and Arthur Middleton, age thirty-four, were made prisoners at the siege of Charleston.

Thirty-eight-year-old Thomas Nelson's home was used as British headquarters during the siege of Yorktown. Nelson reportedly offered five guineas to the first man to hit his house.

Carter Braxton, age forty, lost his fortune during the war.

Forty-two-year-old Thomas McKean wrote that he was "hunted like a fox by the enemy, compelled to remove my family five times in three months."

Forty-six-year-old Richard Stockton was dragged from his bed at night and jailed.

Fifty-year-old Lewis Morris's home was taken and used as a barracks.

Fifty-two-year-old Abraham Clark had two sons tortured and imprisoned on the British starving ship *Jersey*.

More Americans died on British starving ships during the Revolution than died in battle.

Fifty-three-year-old John Witherspoon's son, James, was killed in the battle of Germantown.

Sixty-year-old Philip Livingston lost several properties to British occupation and died before the war ended.

Sixty-three-year-old Francis Lewis's wife was imprisoned and treated so harshly that she died shortly after her release.

Sixty-five-year-old John Hart's home was looted, and he had to remain in hiding, dying before the war ended.

Forty-one-year-old John Adams wrote to his wife of the Declaration, "I am apt to believe that it will be celebrated, by succeeding generations, as the great anniversary festival. It ought to be commemorated, as the Day of Deliverance by solemn acts of devotion to God Almighty. It ought to be solemnized with pomp and parade, with shows, games, sports, guns, bells, bonfires and illuminations from one end of this continent to the other from this time forward forever more."

Adams continued in his letter to his wife:

"You will think me transported with enthusiasm but I am not. I am well aware of the toil and blood and treasure, that it will cost us to maintain this Declaration, and support and defend these States. Yet through all the gloom I can see the rays of ravishing light and glory. I can see that the end is more than worth all the means. And that posterity will triumph in that day's transaction, even although we should rue it, which I trust in God we shall not."

Thirty-four-year-old James Wilson, who signed the Declaration and the Constitution and was appointed to Supreme Court by George Washington, stated in 1787, "After a period of six thousand years since creation, the United States exhibit to the world the first instance of a nation...assembling voluntarily...and deciding...that system of government under which they and their posterity should live."

John Jay, the president of the Continental Congress from 1778 to 1779 and the first Chief Justice of the United States, wrote in 1777:

The Americans are the first people whom Heaven has favored with an opportunity of...choosing the forms of government under which they should live. All other constitutions have derived their existence from violence or accidental circumstances.... Your lives, your liberties, your property, will be at the disposal only of your Creator and yourselves.

Ezra Stiles, the president of Yale, stated in 1788: "All the forms of civil polity have been tried by mankind, except one: and that seems to have been reserved in Providence to be realized in America."

At the time of the Revolutionary War, nearly every country on earth was ruled by a king.

Dr. Pat Robertson wrote in *America's Dates with Destiny* (1986):

On September 17, 1787, the day our Constitution was signed, the absolute monarch Ch'ien Lung, emperor of the Manchu (or Ch'ing) Dynasty, reigned supreme over the people of China.... Revolts were put down by ruthless military force.

In Japan the shogun (warriors) of the corrupt Tokugawa chamberlain Tanuma Okitsugu exercised corrupt and totalitarian authority over the Japanese.

In India, Warren Hastings, the British Governor of Bengal, had successfully defeated the influence of the fragmented Mogul dynasties that ruled India since 1600.

Catherine II was the enlightened despot of all the Russias. Joseph II was the emperor of Austria, Bohemia and Hungary. For almost half a century, Frederick the Great had ruled Prussia.

Louis XVI sat uneasily on his throne in France just years away from revolution, a bloody experiment in democracy, and the new tyranny of Napoleon Bonaparte.

A kind of a constitutional government had been created in the Netherlands in 1579 by the Protestant Union of Utrecht, but that constitution was really a loose federation of the northern provinces for a defense against Catholic Spain....

What was happening in America had no real precedent, even as far back as the city-states of Greece. The only real precedent was established thousands of years before by the tribes of Israel in the covenant with God and with each other.

President Theodore Roosevelt proclaimed in 1903: "In no other place and at no other time has the experiment of government of the people, by the people, for the people, been tried on so vast a scale as here in our own country."

President Calvin Coolidge declared in 1924: "The history of government on this earth has been almost entirely a history of the rule of force held in the hands of a few. Under our constitution, America committed itself to the practical application of the rule of reason, with the power held in the hands of the people."

America is a republic where the people get to rule themselves. If an American disrespects the flag, what that person is in effect saying is that he no longer wants to be king. He wants someone else to rule his life, which is the definition of slavery.

Ronald Reagan opened the Ashbrook Center, Ashland, Ohio, May 9, 1983, with these words:

From their own harsh experience with intrusive, overbearing government, the Founding Fathers made a great breakthrough in political understanding: They understood that it is the excesses of government, the will to power of one man over another, that has been a principal source of injustice and human suffering through the ages.

The Founding Fathers understood that only by making government the servant, not the master, only by positing sovereignty in the people and not the state can we hope to protect freedom and see the political commonwealth prosper.

In 1776 the source of government excess was the crown's abuse of power and its attempt to suffocate the colonists with its overbearing demands. In our own day, the danger of too much state power has taken a subtler but no less dangerous form.

John Adams wrote in 1765, "I always consider the settlement of America...as the opening of a grand scene and design in Providence for...the emancipation of the slavish part of mankind all over the earth."

John Jay noted in 1777:

This glorious revolution...distinguished by so many marks of the Divine favor and interposition...and I may say miraculous, that when future ages shall read its history they will be tempted to consider a great part of it as fabulous...The many remarkable...events by which our wants have been supplied and our enemies repelled...are such strong and striking proofs of the interposition of Heaven, that our having been hitherto delivered from the threatened bondage of Britain ought, like the emancipation of the Jews from Egyptian servitude.

Ronald Reagan stated 1961:

In this country of ours took place the greatest revolution that has ever taken place in the world's history. Every other revolution simply exchanged one set of rulers for another...Here for the first time in all the thousands of years of man's relation to man...the founding fathers established the idea that you and I had within ourselves the God-given right and ability to determine our own destiny.

Henry Cabot Lodge warned his colleagues in the U.S. Senate in 1919, "The United States is the world's best hope.... Beware how you trifle with your marvelous inheritance...for if we stumble and fall, freedom and civilization everywhere will go down in ruin."

Bill Federer captures the tension and complete and total jeopardy into which our Founders willingly put themselves. To read the accounts of the suffering that befell almost all of them is difficult to read. One can only imagine the toll it must take to know that the death of a child, along with the torture and death of a wife, has come from your actions. What our Founders did could be considered pure madness, until you see how history unfolded, and recognize the the gift they gave all of us, even the world.

To be sure, the odds they faced were so terrible, it would have been madness for an atheist to do what they did. As believers in the Almighty God, we can see it was not madness, but faith in divine Providence and belief in a cause more profound than any in history that drove them to take the mad leap.

When no one was looking

While the media were attacking and the swamp monsters were smirking at the prospect of a Donald Trump presidency, Donald Trump and his loyal league of supporters were working away using business and marketing strategies that would produce a surprise on Election Day.

The elite media laughed at the idea that Trump could be president, mocking him and his supporters. Even the more level-headed media treated him like a carnival sideshow—good for ratings, but he could never ever be president. And his base quietly continued their work.

Pre-Trump, I spoke often to Christian and conservative Jewish women's groups. They had always warmly welcomed me—my base, if you will. But as I began to defend Donald Trump, people began trying to cancel my appearances, and a hush would come over a room when I walked into Republican gatherings. One thing was clear: They did not appreciate my supporting Donald Trump for president, and they wanted to be sure I knew that.

For an entire year, I gave speeches to conservative groups, some of whom were hostile because of my support for Trump. Every speech I made that year included my thoughts on Grace, as I believed it was particularly relevant to this race.

I called this speech "Have You Ever Been Wrong?" I wanted to dig into the hearts of an electorate that was so sure Donald Trump could not lead our country. I wanted to shake America and remind her that God sometimes uses unlikely people. Maybe Donald Trump was the person "for such a time as this" (Esther 4:14 NIV).

I shared with my audiences the times I had been wrong so I wouldn't offend them when I suggested that they could be wrong, too. I understood their fear: What if Donald J. Trump was all of those terrible things that the media and establishment said he was? But what if he wasn't?

He had been a Democrat. True. He had a few wives and less than upstanding girlfriends, yes. Alongside his successes and victories were plenty of failures and mistakes. He was a reality TV star, and he had said some things that made one's skin crawl.

But when I found myself standing in judgement, I recognized my own bigotry—and the left's. While calling themselves "tolerant," some are ferociously intolerant.

When I looked more closely at this man, I realized that he had been vetted as no other candidate in history ever was. I knew that had he run as a Democrat, he would have received the same kid-glove treatment the Clintons and Obamas enjoyed.

How to tell when someone is lying to you

In counseling pregnant and post-abortion women, helping them through their struggles and sometimes with their bills, I have undergone intensive truth-detection training, learning to distinguish the subtlest facial expressions, glances, and twitches and to detect holes in stories. I applied these skills to Mr. Trump. I wasn't finding anything that caused me to doubt his sincerity.

True, he had a past. We have all done things we are not proud of doing. But if we are truly tolerant, that shouldn't be an issue. What kept me believing in him was the question of his motivation. Why would he trade being king of the realm at Trump Enterprises for being the target of the most vicious media abuse that any politician has ever received and watching his loved ones go through the same?

I had no answer, except that maybe he not only believed in his mission, but was actually called by God with such force that even he didn't know how to say no.

If he was sincere, then he deserved my support. If he was truly a patriot, might he be the change, the disrupter, that we had been looking for?

Nevertheless, I feared embarrassment. I still do some days. I have spent a lifetime building political capital. I have been disappointed in candidates in whom I have invested my hopes. I didn't want to bet it all on someone only to be disappointed again. So I kept watching. And I kept noticing that he was extremely consistent.

Maybe Donald Trump had experienced enough over a long and eventful career finally to come around, to get his house in order. Maybe he had acquired some wisdom by his eighth decade of life. What if he truly wanted to restore constitutional government? What if he was the man who could save a future for our children?

America was so damaged. Some days, I didn't believe America could be saved. But some days, I could envision a true leader again, one who would put America first, who would be faithful to its constitution, who would transcend the identity politics dividing us, and who would treat our economy like a business and bring back growth and prosperity. When I became convinced that Donald Trump was that leader, I couldn't rest until he was in the White House. I became a one-woman campaign, and I was willing to stand alone.

I studied everything I could to find that would help me defend this candidate from every angle. My husband always tells me, "If you're going to put your name on someone, make sure he *wins*!" And I always tell my children I want three words inscribed on my tombstone: "She died tryin'!"

The great Christian writer C. S. Lewis insisted that, as a matter of logic, you have to believe one of three things about Christ, who said he was God: either he was a liar, he was a lunatic, or he is God.[2] Now Donald Trump does not claim to be divine, of course, but the same logic compelled me to keep making the case that he might have been called by God. That is, either he was megalomaniacal, mad, or a man called by God himself "for such a time as this," perhaps even despite himself.

At first, it was pretty lonely out there, and I could count on one hand my friends who saw what I saw in this larger-than-life man who had entered the arena for what I believed was a cause bigger than himself. Soon, however, the number of those willing to stand with me in that fight began to grow.

But those tweets tho

"I will build a great wall—and nobody builds walls better than me, believe me—and I'll build them very inexpensively. I will build a great,

great wall on our southern border, and I will make Mexico pay for that wall. Mark my words."

"If I were running 'The View', I'd fire Rosie O'Donnell. I mean, I'd look at her right in that fat, ugly face of hers, I'd say 'Rosie, you're fired.'"

"All of the women on The Apprentice flirted with me—consciously or unconsciously. That's to be expected."

"Happy #CincoDeMayo! The best taco bowls are made in Trump Tower Grill. I love Hispanics!"

...and so many more!

After I was appointed to the Donald J. Trump 2020 Media Advisory Board, the first question everyone asked was, "Are you going to advise him to stop tweeting?"

It reminded me of what we call the "s" question in the homeschooling community. When you tell people you homeschool your children, they invariably ask, "How will you socialize them?" I respond with something I read somewhere in my Home School Legal Defense Association paperwork: "If a kid has to get along with his brothers and sisters while eating, cleaning the home, doing school, riding in the car, and working as a unit, do you think he needs stronger or weaker social skills than a kid who goes from class to class each day with an assortment of strangers the same age as himself, exchanging a glance or a smile (or perhaps a smack in the head)?" People just stare at me as they figure out that home schooling is a social skill all its own.

But that is another topic.

Trump's tweets are in fact the secret of his success against the old media. He uses them to play both offense and defense, advancing his agenda and fending off his attackers.

When he's on defense, the art of the tweet works like this:

The media concoct a false narrative. This is nothing new. They did it to Bush, Palin, Reagan… They have done it going back as far as I can remember, but only to conservatives, or Republicans. They scream for tolerance while trying to silence everyone who has a different opinion.

Trump fires off a tweet, usually turning the argument on his attacker.

They respond with an *ad hominem* attack, based on the logical fallacy of rebutting an argument by attacking the character or the motive of the person making the argument.

Trump enjoys the spectacle of the media chasing their tails and exposes their failure to rebut his argument.

The cycle continues...

When he wants to play offense—defining a narrative, changing the news cycle, or speaking directly to his base—the tweet is just as useful.

He sends a tweet, grabbing headlines by using words the media deem "improper" or "unpresidential."

The media almost certainly take the bait, and like sharks on a line, begin to zig and to zag, unaware that the one who cast the line above has limited their scope and efficacy.

The base is encouraged that their man is, once again, shown to be a real guy who wants to speak to them and doesn't care what the elite in the media or Washington say about it. It is his bond with his base. The media will never understand it.

The more outrage the media show, the more the base is encouraged, and the more the president is in control of the sharks, who can only swim back and forth because they refuse to try a new trick.

The cycle continues...

The efficacy of President Trump's tweets became clear to me as I watched him whip the media into a frenzy over and over during the campaign. If his tweets weren't effective, why did those who hate him want so badly for him to stop? If he hadn't been winning with his tweets, they would have kept quiet about them, waiting for him to commit suicide by Twitter. But they were *obsessed*, and this told me that candidate Trump was totally on to them. He was in their heads.

Breitbart reported during the campaign that Trump's Facebook page reached more than 21 billion impressions from the day he kicked off his campaign until he won, totaling more than 50 million likes! His Twitter operation looked equally impressive, garnering nine billion impressions on his feed from June 2015 until Election Day.

The establishment media did what they could to diminish Trump's social media marketing genius. When he had rallies, they would grossly under-report the numbers of those present. So Team Trump would simply take to Facebook Live or Periscope to tell the real story.

The Trump base realized that if the media were lying to them about crowd size, they were probably lying about other things as well.

Print media were already failing, losing money, closing entire divisions, and laying people off. Now, armed with other ways to get the truth, the Trump base's critical thought would cost media severely. Their ratings would drop, their doors would close, and their credibility would be shot. More and more turned to alternative media to find the truth.

In the midst of the campaign, however, it was discovered that some social media sites were actively working against Trump. Hashtags like #deplorables, #maga and #TrumpTrain were trending until Twitter and Facebook succumbed to pressure to use algorithms to distort those trends. But even when the media tried to derail the Trump movement, the movement would find a way around them, like a skier on a slalom course.

Social media seemed as tone deaf as corporate media. Neither seemed to realize that the more they tried to censor, the more they tried to damage, the more they tried to push Donald Trump into a place where he couldn't win, the more likely they made their own defeat. The evidence was everywhere, but it was as though they couldn't do the math.

Trump used Twitter like a general commanding his troops, throwing his enemies off track, taking hostages, getting the enemy to negotiate against themselves.

Trump's masterly deployment of social media to win the election was particularly galling to the left, who consider themselves the natural rulers of the tech world. The internet was Al Gore's invention, after all! This was simply one more way candidate Trump proved the media and all conventional election wisdom wrong.

CHAPTER 3

TRIUMPH BORN OF TRAGEDY

What Happened Along the Way

*"How the hell did you end up a conservative? I thought I
raised you better than that!"*
— *My dad*

Jefferson City is a sleepy little river town where people go to work,
come home, and raise their families. They boat, fish, watch sports,
or hunt on the weekends. It is the capital city of Missouri, though
you would never know it driving through, unless you happened past
the capitol. When I was growing up, it was mostly German Catholic,
and conventionalism seemed to be woven into the very fabric of the
little town. Jefferson City is where I saw my greatest tragedies and
greatest triumphs as a child and young adult. It is also where I cut
my political teeth.

My dad never really fit into the little town that lit up only during the
legislative session each year. He didn't hunt or fish. Most people worked
for the government; but he was the entrepreneur's entrepreneur—a clever
medical inventor who retired young because he made all the money he
would ever need. He was anything but Catholic or conventional. He was
a bodybuilder with a special disdain for spectator sports. He liked to be
in the game, so it made sense that upon his early retirement, he moved

to Corpus Christi, Texas, to live on the water, where he had good wind so that he could windsurf and kite board every day.

I didn't fit into my hometown growing up either, but for different reasons. Children didn't have divorced parents in Jefferson City. Children didn't have single mothers. Children didn't have dating fathers. Children didn't show up for the father-daughter dances without a father. Children weren't only children; they were from big Catholic families with a whole tribe behind them to tell them all the little things I seemed not to know. Children's dads drove station wagons, not motorcycles like my dad.

My family wasn't Catholic, but I went to the Catholic school. I was sure that the people there would be flattered that my family chose to pay the hefty "non-Catholic" tuition, and surely these religious people would respect that I had different views and love me anyway.

My first day of Catholic school, Sister Lucy (also known as Sergeant Lucy) asked if there was anyone in the class that didn't go to mass on Sundays. I quietly raised my hand, as if my silence were a request that the nun might honor and keep it between us. Her forehead furrowed, but she didn't say a word. Whew. I made it through that hurdle, I thought.

Then she asked if there were any only children in the room. Jo Ellen Murphy and I raised our hands. Sister Lucy asked why we were only children. I didn't hear Jo Ellen's answer, because I was racing through possible answers in my mind. I could tell Jo Ellen had been asked that question before, and she had an eloquent response. I didn't. I said that both of my parents were only children, and maybe that was why. I didn't really know. Then I guessed that since my parents were divorced when I was very young, they didn't have time to have more children. That was a bad answer. I watched as Sister Lucy's face became furious and inflamed at my answer. Then she dropped the big bomb.

Sister Lucy took her place center stage of our modest little Catholic school classroom. She widened her commanding stance and belted out her next question in a man voice, "Who in this classroom has parents who were not married in the Catholic Church?"

I felt momentary relief because I figured that I couldn't be the only one whose parents weren't married in a Catholic church. My parents were married in a Christian church. Maybe that would suffice for this nun on an obvious mission that day.

It didn't.

I raised my hand and watched as Sister Lucy approached me in my desk. It felt like she grew and I shrank as she got closer and closer. She stood right at my desk and started in a whisper, "Well you know what that means, don't you?"

"Um, no…?" I managed to utter.

"That means you are a bastard!" she roared over me.

That moment told me that this was going to be a difficult year, and maybe a difficult life within the walls of this school. But I would survive. I was used to being alone and not fitting in. I was so used to it, in fact, that it felt like my comfort zone, in an odd way.

My dad took no great offense to Sister Lucy's behavior that day. But he did take exception to most things I was taught in that school. They had a dress code, and my dad couldn't get over their insistence on modesty. My dad liked to take nudist vacations; he was never one for modesty. He had a very active single life in our little town, and did not approve of any impediment to birth control access. And finally, my dad gave big money to Planned Parenthood because he was for "Zero Population Growth," so he did not appreciate the Catholic pro-life or pro-natalist perspective. My dad designed and distributed bumper stickers that read, "The Ultimate Pollution Solution: Birth Control."

Everything in me wanted to agree with my dad on all things Catholic. I didn't want to be pro-life. I didn't care to observe rote traditions on Sunday mornings when I could sleep instead. I didn't want to be obedient to a God, or anyone else, really. I loved irreverence toward conventionalism. It made me more like my dad. More than anything in the entire world, I wanted my dad's approval. That has never changed.

My dad and I would spend hours in his office listening to Paul Harvey. Then we would debate during the commercials and after the show was over. He would ask what I thought about something Paul Harvey said, and we would talk until we found something we disagreed on, and then we would debate it point by point. By the time I was in junior high,

I doubted every convention and value my conservative mother and my little town had ever instilled in me.

I knew I was a debater by nature and training, so I joined the speech and debate class to show off my skill and get an easy A. The first topic we were asked to debate was abortion. I could pick the side I wanted to defend. But everyone knew who my dad was and presumed I would take the pro-choice side, as did I. That would be easy—I'd explain that the "baby" isn't a baby at all, that the scientific reality is that it is simply tissue, which at some point becomes a baby.

I began my research. I read emotional stories from women who had aborted their babies. I read poems and prayers, and I felt that I knew so much more than these poor, simple souls who believed that something so tiny was actually alive. In my pity for their ignorance, I felt great pride that I would never walk with the simple people, and that I would always be intellectually superior to those who had to rely on some God for comfort and attention.

I remember the moment that rocked me. I was looking for the proof that I was sure existed that an abortion was tantamount to crushing an ant, or pruning a plant, when I read, "thirty days after conception the heart begins to beat."

That couldn't be right.

Thirty days was way too soon. Most people didn't even know they were pregnant by then! Then I recall reading about the development of the nervous system of the baby. Then I read about fingers and toes, and sight and taste and touch. The description of the "fetus" at the age where most are aborted, read very much like the description of a human. This bothered me.

I told myself that the process of abortion was very humane, certainly more humane than bringing an unwanted child into the world.

I read about salt water abortions, and others where babies were sucked into a tiny tube, or delivered and then a scissor was inserted into their little head. I was physically sickened by this. I searched frantically through medical books for the part where they numbed the baby...put the baby to sleep...for crying out loud, did something to mask the pain of being burned to death or sucked piece by piece into a tube. I couldn't find it. It wasn't there. There was no numbing, no painkilling, no masking the pain that baby felt. And that baby was more than an ant or spider. I couldn't kill either bug. So there I stood, face to face with my own hypocrisy. I looked at pictures of abortions, and I just couldn't get past them. No wonder my dad and other friends on his side of this issue found those photos so offensive. I was offended in every way possible.

How was I going to give my pro-choice speech?

I was a liberated, liberal, unconventional, live-by-my-own-rules-or-die kind of girl. I could not go in there and give a right-wing freak-fest speech!

I had my dad write me a doctor's excuse form to miss my speech that day. He tried to explain to me that even though the fetuses might have feelings, we all do. He said the woman has a right to her career or other pursuits without the impediment of a needy, demanding baby clutching her side and weighing her down. I agreed. I had been raised to be completely annoyed by children in every way. Since I had no siblings or cousins, those strange, noisy, sticky little parasites (yes, my dad and I did refer to babies as parasites) were purely annoying.

My dad encouraged me to give my pro-choice speech that day. He knew my love for animals and bugs, so he appealed to my sensitive side that the fetus is better off not being born anyway, because there were too many unwanted babies. He then explained to me that I was one of those. My mother had flushed her birth control pill down the sink despite his insistence he didn't want to populate the earth with any babies. This was part of the reason for the divorce (as well as his inability to turn away other women, and her smoking habit). He also told me that by his belief system, as a purist on these matters, science doesn't really condone the frivolity of useless lives, like people with severe disabilities or those who do not contribute to the human race in some tangible way. He believed in humane euthanasia for those whose lives were miserable, and he confessed that many times he had wished he had been aborted. It would have been more humane, he said, than his mother forcing him to live a life that is often painful and unfulfilling.

I felt my world crumble as I faced the worst demon to date—my inevitable shortcoming and consequent inability to be Daddy's Little Girl. That could never happen now. I saw life as a gift, an endless path of opportunity and possibility. I saw people as sacred. I saw life as a right.

There I had it: Confirmation of my worst fear. I was the reason for my parents' divorce. Worse, if I was to believe that the fetus was created somehow with a right to be born, then I had to wonder who created it. Worse still, if I thought my life was at all worthwhile, I had to face the fact that even unwanted babies might have some intrinsic worth and reason to be born. I hated a lot about what I thought to be my new truth, but I knew one thing: I had to be authentic. My dad, for all his faults, was brutally honest. I had to be that.

I went to school the next day with my posters and my speech, wishing I could disappear. I remember fantasizing that the school burned before it started that day, a tornado warning sounded, or a snowstorm rolled in and school was called off for weeks while I found some solution to my predicament.

It was mildly comforting to know that my speech and debate teacher, Miss Brown, liked me. She might cut me some slack. I began, shaking. I have no recollection of what I said in those eight minutes, but I remember I nailed the timing. I finished to a rousing applause by about half the class, and utter silence from the others, including Miss Brown. She stared at me open-mouthed, as if I had somehow betrayed her by taking the pro-life position that was the fruit of my research. Her anger was palpable.

After a grueling questioning period from Miss Brown, she explained that because I was so narrow-minded and anti-woman, I would be getting a C for the speech, and that perhaps I could be more enlightened next time around.

I was devastated. I guessed that Miss Brown hadn't liked me after all, but had only approved of my politics. I guessed my honor roll streak was over because of this stupid speech. But worse, I realized that I had shattered my own dreams of my father's approval, with no clue how to put it all back together again.

I wanted to die. The single focus of my entire life had been to gain my dad's love, and I knew that I had learned something that day that I could not deny and that would ruin my life forever. I was one of them. I was one of the ones who I had thought were stupid. This had a broad range of implications that scared me to death. This could mean I was a bigot, or a racist, or any number of the horrible things I hated and thought I could never be. This meant I would have to ask questions about the God I wanted to deny. This meant that I would never achieve my goal of gaining my dad's love and approval.

It was all true. I was changed. I was what I feared and hated. I would learn my dad's rejection over and over based on my politics. I would endure the scorn of being a conservative in public, in school, and very personally. And ultimately, I would fall deeper and deeper into my search for authentic truth through the lens of the researcher and scientist my dad had raised me to be.

I learned some very hard lessons over the next couple of years as I tried to adjust to my new lens of life. I had an awesome sophomore year, and I decided to try to give back to this God who my mom had always told me was there. I registered to become a counselor at Camp Wonderland, a camp for the mentally disabled. I was the counselor to a cabin of six of the most amazing men I would ever know. Most of them had Down syndrome. All of them were mentally disabled.

We spent weeks that summer in the Missouri Ozarks fishing, doing crafts, singing and dancing, and celebrating life. They taught me something I had never known about living in the moment and drinking up all life had to offer. They taught me joy. They taught me the spirit of God, and I was forever changed.

I knew from that first day that I wanted that special joy in my life, and if this God didn't give me one of my own, I would adopt. I confessed that dream to one of the mothers of one of my favorite campers as we were all saying goodbye for the summer. I will never forget her response. "Thank God there wasn't abortion back when I had Stanford," she said. "I would have aborted. Anyone would who didn't know how amazing such a simple life can be. There is a whole lot of joy in that chromosomal mutation," she quipped. "He saved my life in so many ways."

She would have lost all that joy if she believed, as I had once, that she would have been better off. Instead, she had this baby who had so touched my life that it was forever changed!

I was still hoping to escape the political truth that I had come to know that fateful day when I went to college. I met a good-looking guy named John, who was a political moderate, a Christian Scientist, and from a nice family in a suburb west of St. Louis. As our relationship became more and more serious, we began to search for the unconventional truth we both aspired to embrace. He was pro-choice, believed Jesus was teacher but not a savior, liked the idea of a strong UN, and shared my passion for unfiltered truth and justice.

We were both voracious researchers on a quest for truth, and neither of us wanted to be a conservative. We went to Buddhist, Islamic, Wiccan, and other "churches" just to avoid the conventional. We took courses by the most liberal professors, hoping to learn something that changed the perspective that seemed to be emerging for both of us. We rescued wolves, pigs, and pit bulls, and we protested fur and meat eating. We poured ourselves into activism that didn't force a political choice, as if we both knew that we were about to make the final, fatal fall into the abyss of conservatism—and Christian conservatism, at that. We knew our lives would probably merge, and we sought desperately to find a way that it wouldn't be conservative or conventional.

I remember the day all of that changed. John was taking a civil liberties class taught by Judge Paul Spinden of the Missouri Supreme Court. Judge Spinden asked John a question: If a girl is pregnant, and someone kicks her and kills the baby, is that murder? John's natural answer was yes. Then Judge Spinden replied, so what, then, is an abortion, if the same girl chooses it, the same day? "Well, that is her choice," John responded.

He heard his own words. He came to me after class convicted and upset. "Gina, you have to help me think of why, if a pregnant woman's baby dies as the result of a person's kicking her, that is murder, but if that same day she decides to abort that baby, it is choice!" He pleaded, "I need you to help me reconcile this!"

I knew his conflict.

We discussed how laws had to be written, despite emotion and personal feelings, and how it seemed to us that the Roe v. Wade decision was bad law.

As we began to embrace the truth as we were seeing it, we began to realize that most people weren't like us. Most people our age believed what was politically correct, and the media were becoming more and more intolerant of dissenting opinions. We began to see ourselves as the rebels, and decided that being conservative was no longer conventional.

John and I married, and I took him to Camp Wonderland to meet the people with Down syndrome who had come to mean so much to me in my search for truth. He loved them too, and that year he took a second job as a teacher to the profoundly mentally disabled in our little college town of Fulton, Missouri. We married in the Westminster Mary Aldermanbury church, where we met four years earlier at a blood drive. Our wedding party included our "campers" with mental disabilities, because we loved them and wanted them in our lives.

Shortly after we were married, John was elected to the Missouri House of Representatives. I got domestic and started searching for a baby with Down syndrome to adopt. I called every Planned Parenthood in our state asking if they would give my name and number to anyone in there who had an unwanted pregnancy with a genetic issue. I searched for ten years, through three babies of my own, and I never one time received a call.

The Up Side of Down: Sam's Story

My mom taught me early in my childhood that even though I love animals, I can't save them all. But I knew if I could save one life, I might somehow be able to mentally withstand the idea of this massive slaughter of the most innocent through abortion.

I can be a slow learner. But it took me almost a decade to learn that Planned Parenthood is not in the adoption business. Their business model doesn't allow for children to go to happy homes, but rather to meet a much more wicked fate. I still wonder how many wonderful little babies with Down syndrome Planned Parenthood killed in the ten years I was praying and searching for a baby with Down syndrome to be part of our lives and our love.

But even in the midst and witness of pure evil, I believe God causes "in all things God works for the good of those who love Him." (Romans 8:28 NIV)

The best laid plans . . .

It was a cold, dark day in the throes of winter in Missouri. I lay on my red leather couch in my suburban home, wondering how I had arrived in the place I was.

My husband's political career was in peril, and he was in the race of his life. Pro-life forces who were supposed to be friends had killed his landmark pro-life legislation because other pro-life groups might get credit, and today he was in the governor's mansion in intense meetings to determine a plan of action. I was lying on a sofa in suburbia carrying a baby that was not supposed to survive.

The question echoed in my mind that I had believed for so many years: If there is no abortion, who is going to take all these unwanted babies?

I am! I wanted to scream. But my desire fell on deaf ears as I approached clinic after clinic, and never one time got the call I had prayed for.

One day, I decided to go beyond Missouri and start calling abortion clinics in other states. It was a lady in Kansas who finally drove the truth home to me after I gave her my name and number and asked if I could send her the little booklet of photos of our family that I had put together for a prospective mother.

"We are not in the business of adoptions," she said coldly. "I suggest if you want an adoption, you call an adoption clinic. We are paid to do abortions."

I was shocked. What about all the babies that were "unadoptable," I wondered. What about the mothers who had nowhere else to turn but abortion, because they thought no one would want their babies? What kind of cold heart wouldn't want to connect a mother in agony to someone willing to take her "unwanted" baby?

That is the moment I came to see the abortion industry as something entirely different.

I called adoption agencies, and they all wanted to help me, but not with an "imperfect" baby. I went to Russia to try to adopt a baby with Down syndrome, but they wanted to send me home with a "proud representation of Russia's intelligence," as the director of one orphanage put it.

One day, when I was calling around to adoption agencies, I asked the lady why they didn't have any children with Down syndrome available for adoption. "They're all aborted today," she said. "Genetic testing has made it so that the only people having babies with Down syndrome are those who decided to keep it even after they know."

I had my answer. Another story I had bet on all my life, destroyed, right along with my dream of inviting one of those little joy-filled guys into our lives. But miracles do still happen.

We continued to pray for that miracle. I believed God had called us to be the parents of a child with Down syndrome. I just had to figure out how to make that happen.

John sponsored pro-life legislation each year for a few years in his Senate tenure, and each year the bill would be killed by his own party and by "pro-lifers" who either wanted credit for the bill or wanted their own bill to pass.

After he had served fourteen years in the House of Representatives and the Senate, John and I felt he was called to take the next political step and run statewide. We were in the campaign of our lifetime. We had two little girls and our first son, and we so loved watching our daughters be "sisters," that we wanted a brother for Jack to complete our family. I lost twin boys and then a single baby, and the campaign along with our work in the Senate was taking its toll on our little family.

I had miscarried before, but wanting a brother for our son, Jack, I was elated to think of twin brothers for him! When we lost the twin boys later in my pregnancy, I was devastated. All alone I buried them in the garden at home while John was in session. I sobbed as I shoveled the dirt, found a little box, and put them in the ground. I thought my neighbors would call the men in the white coats to haul me away if they saw me in that state. That was the lowest of low days.

I called my best friend from high school, Niel, who had just lost her husband in a small plane accident. I will never forget the words she said to me: "Gina, you have to trust me on this one. Remember Joel 2:25: God will 'restore to you the years that the locust hath eaten.'"

I was devastated. How could she quote promises to me, in this vulnerable moment, that I knew God couldn't fulfill? I thought she was my friend, but I would have to be an idiot to rest on some idea that God was going to "restore" twin boys! That was the most ridiculous empty promise she could have said to me, I thought.

With three little ones, I was forced by my perinatologist to stay home the week of my birthday in 2006, because I was pregnant again. I was diagnosed again with a sub-chorionic hemorrhage. In my mind, that meant I would lose this baby, too. John made the trek to the capital. He had important meetings that week with the governor about his bills. He had never asked me not to call before, but this day, my birthday, he asked me not to call him during the day because he would be in intense negotiations on his bill with the governor. "However," he added, "if you have an emergency, call on my cell three times, and I will know it is you and step out to call you."

I was on total bedrest, with a prescription of odd teas from my midwife used by slaves to stave off miscarriage. My little girls worked hard to ensure I stayed on the sofa. They nursed me, made the food, took care of the baby, and tried their best to keep things clean for me.

Lying there, feeling worthless and distraught, I looked at my phone and somehow knew it was going to ring and that the call would be life-changing.

It did. At that moment, the call for which our family had waited for more than a decade had come. There was a baby. He had Down syndrome and several other congenital problems. He probably wouldn't live. He was on a feeding tube and was failing to thrive.

I needed time to think and talk this over. So much was happening to me in that moment. I asked if we could wait a day or two to answer, because, in light of my miscarriages, John's campaign, and his pending full legislative package, I wanted time to let it all sink in.

"No," said the businesslike voice on the other end of the phone. "There is a real possibility this baby won't make it." She went into depth about the baby's congenital illnesses, heart, lung, and hip problems, failure to thrive, and the fact that he was on a feeding tube. "If you decide to sign for his adoption, in all likelihood, you could be signing a death certificate. But at least he will die with parents."

I hung up and called John three times. He called me back, just as promised. I told him the story. I added that I knew it was selfish for me to want to do this and that it could be heartbreaking for all of us to adopt him only to watch him die, but I couldn't bear the thought of his dying alone in the big public hospital with no one to even hold him. Tears streamed, but those days crying felt like my normal state.

John agreed. Firmly he ordered, "Call her back and tell her yes."

"But…" I hesitated. The voices of the nay-sayers ran through my brain like a stock ticker.

"Listen, Gina. This is easy," my wise husband said. "If we don't have room in our hearts and in our homes for this baby, then God does not need me in politics. Now, I have to get back in the mansion because I have the governor's ear, and we are going to get this bill done! Call your mother, put her on the next plane to hold and love that baby, and we will leave day after tomorrow!"

I had never heard him sound so sure of anything—ever.

"Oh, and one more thing," he said. "Congratulations, you are the mother of twin boys again!" Woah. Just like that, God had restored my twin boys as I never believed He could. He was right! I was! That baby inside me was still alive, and there was one waiting for me in Florida! Now all I had to do was fight for their little lives!

One we would name for the historic pastor and John's family name, Robert Brewster (the pastor on the Mayflower—we call him Bo), and the other we would name Samuel, the child we prayed for (1 Samuel 1:27).

By grace, I had my appointment that very day with my perinatologist. I feared her answer about how much it might endanger the baby inside me to go get the one in Florida. I had been on bedrest for weeks now, and I was wheeled into the exam room for an ultrasound and exam.

I will never forget her face in that moment. "Dr. Loudon," she said, "I have never seen this, but your hemorrhage has spontaneously dissipated. I can't diagnose you with any problems at this point in your pregnancy. You are free to walk out of here and go straight to Florida to get that baby! Now, go!"

The agency called to say that there would be a thirty-day wait to take Samuel out of the state. We were back at a new low. If we did this, we would certainly lose the campaign. That wouldn't be fair to all our volunteers who had campaigned for months. We couldn't just walk away from them. But we sure as heck couldn't leave that baby there alone! My mother was there now, at the hospital bonding with him and loving him, and he was improving. We had to go get him.

John remembered that he knew Senator Webster, the author of a bill to save Terri Schiavo, who was slated to be killed (and ultimately was) by her husband, against her family's wishes, because she was lingering in a vegetative state. Our family had been blessed to minister to the senator during that time, and thought it might be worth a call to see if he could help us cut through the government red tape.

As we drove, John was on the phone continuously, searching for a way to bring this baby home in short order. This seemed like the craziest thing we had ever done, but for the very best of reasons. A little boy lay waiting for us in a great big hospital in Florida!

Senator Webster answered John's call with the warmest of hellos, and John told him our story. He said he wanted to make some calls in our behalf, to see if he could "move things along."

We kept driving in the direction of Florida, praying, with one baby inside of me, and the other waiting for us in my mother's arms.

Within hours, Senator Webster called to say we would be free to take Samuel home, his health permitting, within forty-eight hours. Another miracle.

We drove on.

Miracle moments

We arrived to find Samuel safe in my mother's arms, pink, happy, and healthy. Not only was he off the feeding tube, but new tests revealed that he was eating, growing, and thriving! But another miracle awaited us: virtually all his health problems, including his heart and lung problems, had disappeared. Just as the hemorrhage had disappeared only days before. Just as the thirty-day waiting period had disappeared, thanks to Senator Webster. Just as God had promised, He was providing in ways beyond my wildest prayers!

Walking out of that hospital was a surreal moment. Holding that tiny preemie in the palm of one hand felt right. Holding him with both arms was total overkill. He was the size of a puppy. But on we walked, quietly, for fear of someone's changing his mind. I can't describe the feeling of holding a baby I didn't bear, but was mine, while holding another inside my belly. It was supernatural in ways we will only experience in moments of life and death.

We brought Samuel home to the waiting arms of his brothers and sisters after only a week. His brother, Bo, was born happy and healthy and loved him from day one. I will never forget the day that the court officer said the words, "Samuel, welcome to your forever family. You may take him home." I still cry when I write those words. Our lives were forever changed.

My plan at that point was to reject those who rejected Samuel. "The people who could reject someone with Down syndrome deserve their own kind of rejection," I reasoned. But God had other plans for that, too.

Samuel has taught me grace for the unforgiving, love for the hateful, and hope for the hopeless. Samuel doesn't focus on those who don't love him. He is fixed on the love he sees, and he finds joy in things I could never appreciate before. He taught me to love the unlovable, and I think we in politics have a lot to learn from my Samuel.

Inside the liberal mind

"He is a very shallow critic who cannot see the eternal rebel in the heart of a conservative."
—G. K. Chesterton

While John worked late nights in his capitol office as a senior senator, I earned two master's degrees and a PhD, and educated my children in his senate office. I read history and philosophy voraciously, and combined them with the science I already knew. We also studied Christian doctrine; John left Christian Science, and we became Calvinists together. My social, spiritual, and philosophical underpinnings were secured in my conservatism, but I needed to go all-in on the economic philosophy if I was to embrace conservatism with full knowledge and authenticity.

Unlike most conservatives I know, I was a social conservative well before I was sold on the fiscal side of conservatism.

I studied economics, and one question burned in my mind: If liberals can embrace "survival of the fittest" in biology, then why can't they embrace the same in economic policy? Although, it wasn't until I met Dr. Jonathan Haidt years later that I was able to put that idea in such succinct terms. It was the years of my dad's trying to convince me of evolution that opened my eyes to the miracle of the marketplace. I was full circle now. I was a conservative all the way through.

After John's terms in the Missouri legislature, I entered the Tea Party in hopes of slapping the establishment Republicans that I resented more than the Democrats. Again, I felt the comfort of being the misfit I fancied myself to be. I enjoyed the rebellion against conventionality and being a part of what was quickly becoming a very powerful movement.

It was natural, then, that I would do on radio and television what I had always loved most about time with my dad—debating the issues. I was fearless on the air, because I knew the issues so well from both sides, and I never had a desire to be right—only to find truth.

I have always had a passion to find truth and communicate it in the most honest way I can. I figure that even if most who know me disagree with me, if we can speak about it honestly, we can come to some truth and do some good together.

I believe in this political concept more strongly than any other, and though I don't have my dad's approval, I do have my dad to thank for giving me the courage of my convictions and an appreciation for civil discourse. I owe him for teaching me that I can love those I disagree with, and that we can find something we agree on that is worth fighting for.

Never was this more apparent than after my career began to take off, and I made an appearance on a reality show on ABC.

An angry tweet from a viewer whom I now know as my friend Xander implied that my Christianity was only skin deep. Thanks to what I learned from my father, I was able to find common ground with this gay man from New York City through an exchange on Twitter, 140 characters at a time.

Xander's political views have evolved, and our relationship is founded on a mutual respect that is so much easier and more powerful than hate and disregard.

I am not a follower of Rick Warren, but I love this statement of his:

> Our culture has accepted two huge lies. The first is that if you disagree with someone's lifestyle, you must fear or hate them. The second is that to love someone means you agree with everything they believe or do. Both are nonsense. You don't have to compromise convictions to be compassionate.[1]

I recently visited my dad for the first time in four years, and took him a copy of my previous book, in which I told the story of Xander in depth.

My father's wife had recently died of cancer, and he was at a low point in his life. I needed him to know that even though it might not have been what he meant to teach me, his influence on my professional life is profound.

I sat next to him at his breakfast table overlooking the intercoastal waterways he enjoys on his kite board each day, and I watched him read my book while I wrote this one on my computer.

He was very sad to learn how much I need that he can't supply in my life. He corrected me on some inconsequential details in the book. I still don't think he understands the extent of his influence on my professional life, or how potent is my quest for truth and common ground with others is because of the relationship I so desire with him.

My mom died recently, and I'm still hoping to be a "Daddy's Girl," more now than ever.

Not everyone can have the degree of testing of truth in his life that I have experienced, and not every journey is as illuminating to the traveler as mine seems to me. I don't fancy myself to be right, only relentless in my search for absolute truth and justice and in my desire to love those who disagree with me and find common ground.

In that spirit, it is my fervent hope that we can transcend the anger and division that pervade our culture right now and build something better, before it is too late.

And I believe in miracles. I have no excuse not to believe. And I find myself now in this place where I have no excuse, but to share an even more personal story that is really the one I go back to in my mind in every political moment of my life. This is how it began...

Confessions: Triumph Born of Tragedy in My Life

"She is barefoot on the beach. She shoots in stilettos."
—What Women Really Want (2014)

I knew where my stepdad kept his little pistol. It was tucked neatly inside an orange box in the top of his bedroom closet. When my parents weren't home, I spent many lonely hours as an only child learning how that gun worked. I wanted one of my own. But in my little town, with its mixture of Southern and Midwestern cultures, girls didn't really do that. So I never asked, for fear my parents would know that I found their gun and had been playing with it when they were away.

In those solitary hours, I loaded and unloaded it. I read and studied about guns, and even drew them. To me, guns were fascinating...they were jewelry, but they were useful. They had mad powers to save and to kill, when in the hands of different people.

I loved the metal, the way it smelled, and the power it represented. I needed power. I had very little power against the politics taking place in my town.

I was in the seventh grade, and our little town was about to learn about corruption, racism, and violence in ways it never planned.

A local preacher had an idea of how to raise more money. He made a lot of money (millions, in fact) preaching about the disadvantaged poor in the inner city and raising money from well-intended folks to "help" these disadvantaged minorities, subject to the gangs and other inherent problems. He wanted to conduct a social experiment in our little river city. He decided that, although we had a black university right there in the town, we were not diverse enough. He reportedly thought the answer was to go to the inner cities and offer these single mothers and their children something better—a home in a little river town and one thousand dollars.

The problem was that the thousand dollars didn't last long, even as a supplement of the welfare system. The victims of his social experiment were used to the big city life. Many of the children were much older than others in their grades, and much larger.

Anything but equal

I made three distinct mistakes that, in the mind of a kid who believed she was a victim, were unforgivable. That meant I needed to pay.

The first and most horrid thing about me was that I was white. I embodied the person they had been taught to hate, the person they believed all their lives was responsible somehow for all their woes.

Secondly, I was small, around ninety pounds. That made me an easy target that they didn't think posed much threat.

Thirdly, I modeled, and made decent money doing it. For some reason, that gave them special venom for me, because they mentioned it all the time. It didn't help that my family drove nice cars and gave me nice clothes that I wore to school. I was "The Advantaged." They didn't know that my dad, like many of theirs, was gone. They didn't know that I woke up many mornings, just as many of them did, feeling inadequate because I wasn't worth staying for. They never thought about how much we were alike. They saw only my material world, and that made me a target of an angry subculture turned gang, growing week by week in my junior high school.

I am not sure what that preacher was hoping to accomplish, but he brought violence, hate, and strife in a town that really wasn't racist—on either side—beforehand. Our little town had always been heralded as one of the most tolerant small towns in the country. I was raised with this as a value, and it made me proud that our town had a culture you wouldn't find in other small towns.

At first, they just robbed me and knocked me around a little. Then they began to employ the rumor mill and threaten my friends and everyone else to stay away from me. I was targeted, and dehumanized in their ranks. They began to follow me everywhere, even into the restroom, or walking places after school. Most of the time they just shouted insults at me, or stole my things (necklaces, earrings, purses, etc.). I was afraid to tell my family, so I would simply say that I lost all my nice things and take the punishment that came.

They threatened to come in the night and slit my mom's throat or kill my dog while she was outside if I told a soul. For some reason, I thought that if I told my mom, she would call the police, and that would make the situation worse.

The gang violence I endured worsened with every success I encountered, and it was beginning to take a toll. Though my family was actually hardworking and middle-class, I was singled out as the "the rich girl," and when any good came my way, I knew I would pay.

When I made the cheerleading squad, I was surrounded by them in an alley and beaten while parents of gang members (parked around the lot where their children were doing the deed), who evidently helped organize the gang beating, cheered for them to "beat the crap outta that rich girl" or "make that rich bitch bleed!" I recall one mother yelling from the car for her son to "F— her like she's your slave!" Another, the biggest girl, who was sixteen years old and six feet tall in the eighth grade, told me she was going to "bust up my pretty face" so she could have my "white boyfriend."

I had just blossomed from queen of the nerd herd that year, and I had grown into my body and my looks enough to be called something other than nerd. That, along with the money they perceived my family had, was reason enough for this gang to hate and threaten me time after time. She did bust up my face, more than once. I told my family that I fell off the top of a pyramid cheerleading.

One day when a few of the gang members pushed me against my locker because they wanted me to go in the bathroom and give them my new sweater, I told them I stole my parents' gun, and so they better be careful.

They immediately went hopping down the hall yelling, "she has a gun, she's gonna kill all us!" They ran straight to the administrative offices and told them that I had a gun. I was in big trouble for that lie, but I wished I had some way to protect myself. Worse than the trouble I was in for threatening to have a weapon, was the fear of being found out, now that the gang knew I didn't have a weapon. I worked out every day, and worked in a gym as a fitness instructor. I learned martial arts, including some weaponry from an Asian friend who knew Jujitsu and was determined to help me defend myself against this hell. But with all my five-feet-one-inch physical strength, I knew I couldn't realistically resist a gang of 150-pound, sixteen- and seventeen-year-old gang members with knives and other weapons.

My family went out to dinner every night after they closed their shops. My mother, a nurse, had the hearing aid shop on the corner downtown, and my grandparents had the uniform and medical equipment shop next door. Grandma—I called her Necie—also sold mastectomy prosthetics and special bras for women who had breast cancer in the back corner of her store. She loved making women feel whole and beautiful again, and no one could do that quite like my grandma. She did that over and over for me.

She was there for me after my parents' divorce, when I was taunted for being the nerd, and now she would be there as I blossomed and became a target for my blessings.

One night as I was walking from cheerleading practice to the restaurant where my family would meet for dinner, I heard voices and hoots. They were coming for me. I prayed that elevator would hurry, and my heart started its familiar racing and pounding. They were there, all around me in the darkness of that parking garage. A rock hit the side of my head, and I felt the familiar cold drip of blood from my ear down my shoulder, all over my new sweater. I wanted to cry but I bit my lip and prayed instead.

"Ding!" the elevator assured me, and its doors opened. Just as I stepped on, one boy stepped inside, too. He began to lick my neck with me cornered, and he smeared my blood all over his chest. He ripped my sweater aside so that my shoulder was exposed, and he kissed my shoulder and then licked it again, violently, like a demon. He grabbed between my legs hard, like he was trying to hurt me. Then felt all over me with his hands. I was frozen.

When the door opened, I walked off. I was afraid even to go to the bathroom alone. The female gang members were scarier in some ways than the males, and I was terrified one would be in the bathroom when I got there.

I did my best to clean up, and grabbed my grandma's suit jacket from the coat hanger as I walked into the restaurant. Though my head had bled a lot, when it stopped, you couldn't see it. I couldn't eat dinner that night, and my mom knew something wasn't right.

I couldn't tell her. They had assured me they would kill my mother if she called the police. I felt completely alone. The gangsters had hurt or threatened any friends I had, and they were all afraid. Even the teachers looked at me like a pariah, knowing that if they did anything to help me, their homes, purses, or children would be terrorized. This gang had single handedly traumatized me. I didn't know how, but they would pay.

The drama came to a climax one day when I was walking to a deli downtown to meet a friend, and the gang came out of dozens of hiding places in an alley and surrounded me again. They wanted the new Gucci handbag that my grandma had given me for my birthday. This time I was feeling bold, and I refused to hand it over, as I had all my jewelry for the past year inside. I really liked this handbag, and my grandma had worked so hard to get it for me, so I wanted to keep it. I had a special love for my grandma. I was her only granddaughter, and she adored me. She would work extra just to buy me special things, and I knew that. It is true that my family had enough money, but my parents and grandparents all worked very hard, usually six days a week. They earned the money we had, and I didn't take that lightly.

I held on to the purse when they grabbed the handle and started pulling me. I kicked and punched back for the first time ever, and I held on. The purse was high quality, and it wasn't breaking. I was hoping they would run off with just the handle if I could hang on to the purse while they dragged, kicked, and punched me into a fetal position around my new handbag from my grandma.

My whole body was raw from being dragged all over the pavement. The skin on my torso was mostly torn away. I never let go of the purse. They left me lying and bleeding in an alleyway, with my shirt almost completely off. I called my mom to come get me and I told her what happened. In parting the gang told me that the next time they were going to kill me. I ended up with a staph infection that had to be treated in the hospital, but the psychological scars would take years to go away.

My parents were irate. They called my godmother, my dad, my grandparents, and our pastor to our home to strategize about what to do.

Searching for solutions

We called on our friends in the black community to help. But they were being terrorized by the same gangs in other ways, and they were afraid to make waves. We went to the black pastors, but they were also afraid of these gangs coming in and exacting violence on their members or vandalizing their property in retaliation. We went to my principal. He told us that his home had been vandalized multiple times, and that the mothers and older siblings of some of the students had threatened his life and his wife's and daughter's, so he admitted his hands were tied. We had nowhere to go. Our town felt like a prison, and I wanted to escape.

Home schooling was not even a thought in those days, so that topic never arose as a potential solution. There was only one other high school in town, and it was Catholic. So even though I wasn't Catholic, and the tuition was extra high for non-Catholics, my parents decided that was probably the safest bet. The Catholic principal assured us that they would not accept any of the gang members into the school on charitable scholarships, so we felt relatively secure in that decision.

I stole my stepdad's gun and carried it and a pocket knife with me to school every day. I no longer cared if I was caught —I believed I would die if they got me alone again unarmed. We counted the days I could miss at the end of the year without a truancy report, and I attended a couple more weeks of school with meticulous plans. My family and other friends of our family picked me up at the door after school. I couldn't go anywhere in our small town without someone there to protect me. One day my grandpa, escorting me out of the school at the appointed time, even ended up in a pushing match with one of the gangsters who was trying to steal my necklace.

That summer, word got out that I was leaving the public school and my friends to attend the Catholic high school. Some people thought it was because my best friend was going there, but many knew in their hearts why I was going—to avoid the brutality and violence of the gang.

Other families moved away, and at least one other well-to-do family put its daughter in the Catholic school.

I was angry. I had long dreamed of attending the public school and being a football cheerleader there. But as the summer wore on, I began to make friends and look forward to my new school.

I stopped taking the gun with me. I had a new boyfriend, who was huge, and I felt safe with lots of friends around me who had no idea about my torment. I had a new start!

Face to face with Satan

One day, I was at my grandma's shop and she needed me to run an errand downtown. I shuddered, but I knew I needed to prove to myself that I was safe now. I wanted to believe my days being brutalized by that gang were over. I wanted to move forward. Besides, there was no way the gangs could get me, I reasoned. They wouldn't even know I was walking, and I would avoid the allies just in case.

As I walked past the area where most of the violent attacks had occurred, my heart raced. I tried to calm myself, but I couldn't. I wished I had my gun. In that moment, I felt a hard thud on the back of my head, and that was all I knew until I woke up in an abandoned building, hoping it was all a dream.

It wasn't. They were madder than ever because some of them had been removed from school over the previous incident, and they were planning to get their revenge with me.

And so the nightmare became my reality. I had no escape. They violated me in the most horrible of ways, for hours, shouting racial slurs at me and laughing about what they had just done to this white girl. I never told a soul. They said this was my payback for telling on them in the first place. They said the cops wouldn't do anything anyway because they had threatened all of them, too. They said if I told anyone, they would come in the night and kill my family, and my dog, and I believed it.

That moment made me realize that I was a true victim of hate. I was a true victim of discrimination. I had no way to legally protect myself from another attack. The only solace I had in that moment, was the fact that my stepdad had that gun, and if they came to try to kill my family, I knew my stepdad or I would use it. That moment made me long for freedom from the slavery I endured. That moment made me want to understand my rights as an American. That moment made me want to be equal.

Lack of equality = Rape

Fast forward ten years.

I was in grad school taking night classes at St. Louis University, because I worked during the day. There had been two rapes on my campus, precisely in or around the building where most of my night classes were held. I had to park blocks away and walk to and from school at night.

My classroom building was flanked by a halfway house for recovering gang members and the Salvation Army. I gave to the Salvation Army, but I also knew how this could all go down: a destitute, addicted gang member decides to rape a privileged co-ed because she has what he doesn't have. I wasn't going to be that headline.

The girls in my grad school and I talked about what to do. We weren't allowed to carry a gun because the university was a "gun-free zone." I bought and carried a stun gun, and I displayed it when I stopped to give beggars money. I wanted them to know I was armed. I was never hurt. But sure enough, only a couple of weeks later, a girl was raped in the darkness right beside my building. She was unarmed.

I vowed in that moment that for the rest of my life, when I was alone, I would be armed.

Equality = Triumph

Fast forward now a few more years. I was working as a talk show host, author, and journalist who dealt with issues regarding guns every day. I was now trained and articulate about the Second Amendment, mass shootings, and even the psychology of the confrontation. I had defended Second Amendment rights in speeches to thousands of people, on national television, and in books I had written. My family was now living in California, and I was cast on the reality show Wife Swap. The folks on Wife Swap were shocked that my daughter and I wanted to go shooting together, and they thought their audience would find that appalling.

They used the footage of me shooting as if it were a sign of lacking compassion. They contrasted me at the range with my daughter, shooting, with footage of one of his women, a wife (the husband in our episode was "polyamorous"—he had more than one woman living with him with no visible obligation to one), breaking into tears squealing "I never want to do it again!" as she shot a gun for the first time. They portrayed me as a calloused, gun-toting, insensitive conservative who wanted to push her Constitution, her Bible, and her guns at everyone else. They quoted me saying, "I don't think the government should regulate how many guns I own. People are afraid of the guns, so they just want to throw them all away. Well the problem is that the criminals will always have guns. I am a five-foot, one-inch petite female. My equalizer is my pistol."

They might have been trying to start a firestorm, but as I have every time someone has tried to make my life difficult, I learned something critical for something I accomplished later.

My gun is my equalizer.

It wasn't my equalizer only when confronted with physical violence. It was my equalizer when someone tried to tell me I was a sexist, a racist, a homophobe, a xenophobe . . . the works! My understanding of the Second Amendment had led me to exactly where I was today and had given me an indisputable argument for equality—that of freedom!

I realized that my enemies, the racists and bigots who had tried to make me their victim, had instead set my life on a trajectory that would be their own undoing, and the very stairway to my success!

The Wife Swap episode showed me saying I was a believer in Jesus Christ overlayed by a loud "bang!" from my rifle, and me defending my pistol as my "equalizer." Instead of the onslaught of hate mail that the producers may have hoped for, I had volumes of mail from women saying they had been victimized in various ways, and before they saw me on Wife Swap, they never understood how integral our Bill of Rights is to our equality.

The preacher who thought he was going to line his pockets on the backs of poor, angry city kids is still in my little hometown—and still getting wealthy, as far as I know. If he thought he was going to curb racism by force, it didn't work, I can assure you. The whispers I heard from the other kids who were victimized, the other kids and their parents who knew what happened, are not repeatable. But rest assured, his legacy is flourishing racial strife. But not in my heart. I won't become a victim that way.

Turmoil = Triumph

I had to ask myself at one point if I was a racist. I learned all about institutional racism in grad school, and I was told over and over that I was a racist because I am (mostly) white, whether I wanted to face that or not, without anyone even knowing the brutality I suffered at the hands of minorities. It's funny—I never really felt much but pity for those who assaulted me. I was filled with rage at the white preacher who created the situation by dropping the gang members into our tiny town with all their anger and blame. I was angry at the white teachers and politicians who constantly told these black kids they were victims and somehow incapable of rising above their circumstances by acting honorably. I was angry at the white administration who were too gutless to protect a child from relentless horrors. I was angry at white kids who watched it all happen and didn't want to "get in the middle of it." I was angry. But it had little to do with color.

I was on a bus tour a couple of years ago with a somewhat notable conservative black activist. I decided to share my story, for the first time, with her. She was as cold as ice about it. Maybe she didn't hear me, or she had her own issues. Whatever her reason, I felt like my painful story didn't resonate. I was hoping to help her understand how someone who had been hurt by racial violence could think on a deeper level than skin color. She didn't seem moved. I decided not to share my story again publicly, until now. Most of my friends and family don't know what I just told you. Thank you for giving me this victory over all of it in this moment.

Am I racist as a result of the torture I endured at the hands of black people?

No. I won't let the haters make me something I am not and never will be. If someone wants to call me that, it doesn't make it so. I have been called worse, I am sure. As the mother of a minority, disabled child, I think it's a pretty tough argument to make. So I laugh when I am called those names.

I do believe that the gang members who hurt me were racist. Most of them are probably dead today. Or worse. I would lay bets that none of them ever rose out of the poverty that that preacher and the rest of society subjected them to. Poverty and anger are slavery. The slave masters today just have cleaner hands, but they are no less guilty. They broke up their families promising to replace them with government handouts. They promise "free stuff" to the vulnerable with the aim of gaining power for themselves. They still enslave, they still harm, they still kill. And I will fight them civilly in the political arena until my dying breath, because my life was designed to be poured out for freedom and equality for all of God's creation.

People ask me all the time how I find the energy to fight day after day against a system that is still dehumanizing, still enslaving people in some ways, breeding violence and strife and sexism and racism and the rest. I say I can fight today because I have been fighting since I was a little girl. I am, in a strange way, thankful that I learned such enormous strength and tenacity as a child. I am thankful, even, that I handled it all alone. There is no question that it has helped make me fearless and independent today. When someone ignorantly decides that I have lived a sheltered life, and that is why I am a conservative, I can laugh inside.

Am I mad? Yes. I am madly in love with life and the promise of Heaven. I am madly obsessed with reaching over to the other side of the aisle in all my clumsy ways and loving those who are willing to let me in. I am madly determined to preserve and protect our precious rights enumerated in our Bill of Rights. I am madly devoted to my children, my family, my true friends, my president for his tireless work to preserve our freedom, and the future of this great nation. I am madly in love with a Savior who still calls to me. And I believe that you have the same madness in you, for such a time as this.

CHAPTER 4

A DEEP DIVE INTO CRAZY

My Journey Through the Insanity That Sparked the New Era of Politics

*"The Right has taken Saul Alinsky's Rules for Radicals
and shoved it up where #TheResistance don't shine."*
—Kurt Schlichter, Townhall.com

"**Y**ou're crazy!" my friend Jane told me. "I don't know you!"

Jane was a true friend, and her concern for me was warranted. I had studied for years to be a business psychologist. When I wasn't studying for a career, I had been campaigning—for friends, for people I believed were fighting for all the right things, and for my husband. Jane couldn't understand why I would throw it all away.

My husband, John W. Loudon, served fourteen years in the House and Senate in Missouri. People thought our lives were glamorous, and maybe they were, but all I could remember were the relentless jabs—unfair and fictitious—from the press. My husband made one crucial mistake: He was a conservative. That was a hanging offense, and most of my adult life was spent trying to navigate around the media to communicate with the people my husband represented—his voters.

It was enough to make me crazy. The false accusations and the constant contention while I was trying to build a family, establish a career, and maintain a home and marriage—it was exhausting. One particularly horrid day, when there was an attack in the eleventh hour of a campaign, I decided I couldn't take it anymore. I thought maybe I would take up smoking. I wasn't much of a drinker, I was afraid of drugs, I was too vain to eat my way into oblivion, and I had no patience for more constructive outlets like exercise. My racing mind told me that if I only had a habit to reduce anxiety, maybe I could better handle the daily storms in the life of a political wife.

I bought a pack of cigarettes and climbed onto the hood of my Honda CRX. I wasn't exactly James Dean, but I felt so rebellious! After a single cigarette, however, I realized this experiment in rebellion was a failure. I couldn't even inhale. Choking and sputtering, I had to face another reality: I had failed to become a smoker. Who does that?

I had met Jane that year. She had held my hand through the highs and lows of life as a political wife raising five children in my husband's senate office so I could be his press secretary. I was a hamster on a wheel. She watched as I nursed an infant in the office before confronting a press gaggle over his latest bill to save a baby or free the midwives. Every day was the definition of crazy.

I responded to both his angry and supportive constituents, ran his campaigns, ironed his shirts, raised and educated his five babies, arranged his travel, wrote his speeches, hired his staff, kept his home and office, handled his press, organized his fundraisers, proofed his letters, and tried desperately to insulate him from most of it.

After fourteen years of winning and losing and fighting to do it all again, I was done.

I saw an escape hatch, and I crawled through it, with a white-knuckle grip on my husband and family. We would do the unthinkable—we would walk away from politics in the prime of our lives.

"The only way to deal with an unfree world is to become to absolutely free that your very existence is an act of rebellion."
—Albert Camus

The adjustment to post-political life was excruciating. It was our drug; our only sense of home. While all our friends were building businesses and careers, we had been campaigning and serving. Like newly released convicts, we had no idea how to live "on the outside." But then a phone call came that would change our lives.

It was from a man named Bill Hennessy, retired Navy, a psychological savant of sorts who worked in marketing. He wanted me to be part of a new project he was calling the Tea Party, taking his cue from the band of Boston patriots who sparked the American Revolution. Bill's latter-day rebellion sought independence from the media, from establishment politics, from the leftist domination of the political narrative. We would call people out of their recliners and into the streets and lead a revolution.

It would take time, Bill warned. He knew the revolution wouldn't happen overnight. But he knew where to start, how to disrupt. He knew public sentiment was with us, even if it was hidden in the living rooms of the heartland. It was there, and we would find it.

Within weeks, we were meeting with Andrew Breitbart, Steve Bannon, James O'Keefe, Jim Hoft—people (like me) whom no one had ever heard of but who shared a deep frustration, not only with the left but also with the right. They wanted to overthrow the power elite, as we did. This was no small task. In fact, it would be monumental. We knew it would be long, painful, ugly, frustrating, and that we could lose. But we all agreed that we had no choice. We were losing our country.

I briefed my loyal friend Jane.

"You're crazy!" She exclaimed. "You have fought so hard for so long! You can't expend all your political capital for some crazy revolution idea! Stay in politics and fight within the system, as you have. That's how to win. Reform the system from the inside. You can't be some silly street-kissing, bull-horn-blowing revolutionary! That's ridiculous."

It was ridiculous. But it was also the beginning of a groundswell that would change the course of history. I was one little cog in the machine, but I was there.

That movement would swell and sway, it would ebb and flow, it would be ridiculed and attacked, but it would culminate in something epic. Instinctually, I always knew we would win. All we wanted was our country back—a noble goal. If Washington and his men could march shoeless through the snow leaving a trail of blood, we could take to the streets with our bull horns and our cell phones, confront the lies, confound the haters, and give the radical left a taste of its own medicine. Ultimately, I believed, God was on our side.

Bullhorns and believers

In 1971, Saul Alinsky, the original "community organizer," composed a tactical manual for the left that became one of the most influential political works in American history—*Rules for Radicals*. Guided by this canny genius, progressive activists did their best to "fundamentally transform" America, as his most famous disciple would put it. Within a generation, Alinsky's radicals had become the establishment, and that's what made them vulnerable to opponents using the same tactics.

Alinsky boiled those tactics down to thirteen simple rules:

1. "Power is not only what you have, but what the enemy thinks you have." Power is derived from two main sources—money and people. "Have-Nots" must build power from flesh and blood.
2. "Never go outside the expertise of your people." It results in confusion, fear and retreat. Feeling secure adds to the backbone of anyone.
3. "Whenever possible, go outside the expertise of the enemy." Look for ways to increase insecurity, anxiety, and uncertainty.
4. "Make the enemy live up to its own book of rules." If the rule is that every letter gets a reply, send 30,000 letters.

You can kill them with this because no one can possibly obey all of their own rules.

5. "Ridicule is man's most potent weapon." There is no defense. It's irrational. It's infuriating. It also works as a key pressure point to force the enemy into concessions.

6. "A good tactic is one your people enjoy." They'll keep doing it without urging and come back to do more. They're doing their thing, and will even suggest better ones.

7. "A tactic that drags on too long becomes a drag." Don't become old news.

8. "Keep the pressure on. Never let up." Keep trying new things to keep the opposition off balance. As the opposition masters one approach, hit them from the flank with something new.

9. "The threat is usually more terrifying than the thing itself." Imagination and ego can dream up many more consequences than any activist.

10. "The major premise for tactics is the development of operations that will maintain a constant pressure upon the opposition." It is this unceasing pressure that results in the reactions from the opposition that are essential for the success of the campaign.

11. "If you push a negative hard enough, it will push through and become a positive." Violence from the other side can win the public to your side because the public sympathizes with the underdog.

12. "The price of a successful attack is a constructive alternative." Never let the enemy score points because you're caught without a solution to the problem.

13. "Pick the target, freeze it, personalize it, and polarize it." Cut off the support network and isolate the target from sympathy. Go after people and not institutions; people hurt faster than institutions.[1]

Using *Rules for Radicals*, the left had set the terms of American politics and culture for decades. Our plan was to turn it on them.

Armed with cell phones and passion, we clumsily pursued this whole disruption thing. The truth is, we weren't very good at it. In our movement's infancy, we were young and dumb and too privileged to be rugged.

Every group wants a leader, but as self-proclaimed "Tea Party leaders" presumed to take the reins of our movement, we learned that real leaders don't appoint themselves. They rise. We also knew that if we chose a leader early on, our movement would be easy to decapitate. We decided we would wait on a leader and just keep learning, fighting, and building.

So on a bitterly cold and rainy Midwestern day, we ditched our establishment microphones and sound systems in favor of a bull horn and loose tea to dump into the Mississippi River. Five hundred people showed up. We knew we could build on that. We shocked ourselves when park rangers told us we had amassed ten thousand Tea Partiers at one rally. We had a movement! What would we do now? Unsure of ourselves but determined to play in the big leagues, we puffed up our protestor chests and tried to devise a plan.

Like all good revolutionaries, we took to a pub when we wanted to seriously strategize. We confronted politicians at their town hall meetings, we made signs and protested local waste, fraud, and abuse. We marched in the streets, and we soon attracted the ridicule (attention and ink) of the local press. That was something. But to change a country, we needed national recognition.

I remember when a Fox News anchor first uttered the words "Tea Party" on the air. We had dreamed of the day we were legit enough to be mentioned by the networks. That day had come. But we knew better than to stop. We had to keep building.

Around that time, a chain of organic grocery stores targeting America's most politically correct shoppers was taking the nation's tonier neighborhoods by storm. Whole Foods Market seemed an unlikely source of opposition to the centerpiece of President Obama's legislative agenda, but its co-founder and CEO, John Mackey, published an op-ed in the *Wall Street Journal* sharply critical of Obamacare. "[T]he last thing our country needs is a massive new health-care entitlement that will create hundreds of billions of dollars of new unfunded deficits and move us much closer to a government takeover of our health-care system," he wrote.[2]

My husband, now working in the private "suit" sector, came home from work wearing his starched white shirt and carrying his briefcase and informed me that he had noticed that unions were picketing Whole Foods.

John knew their tactics. As a senator, he had kicked up a media storm when he changed the name of the Labor Committee, of which he was the chairman, to the Small Business, Insurance, and Industrial Relations Committee. The union rank and file just wanted to feed their families, but the union bosses, as corrupt as the worst CEO, detested my husband for his free-market approach to business.

John knew the unions better than anyone. They would be out in full force with their angry signs and twenty-foot-tall inflatable rats, but he knew there was a way to turn the narrative right back on them.

"Want to go cross their picket line?" he asked me.

I thought for a moment.

Yes. Yes I did. But I wanted to take the ten thousand people from that week's Tea Party with me.

Putting on my business psych hat, I tried to think how to make a marketing statement and define a narrative, Alinsky-style, but for the good guys. I sent out an email asking patriots to join me in two days at our local Whole Foods, bring fifty dollars in grocery money, and see if we could make a difference. That day, my "*Buy*cott" was born.

We spent fifty thousand dollars that night in one Whole Foods store. National news networks took note, and my life changed forever. I would take my Buycott across the country in support of the free market and the rule of law. I would start my national television career and be offered my first radio show, which was later syndicated. My family would move five times in five years, and life would be full of adventure, challenge, passion, and God-breathed miracles!

Mad skills of #WAR

We rallied, we protested, we confronted politicians, we talked to press, and, reluctantly, we occasionally *became* the press.

A guy named Andrew Breitbart mentored many of us. Some of us "stuck," as my grandma used to say, and Breitbart News was born. I was a founding writer for them. We had no idea that one day they would be one of the most influential media outlets in the world. We just wanted to be a voice for those not heard and talk back to the powers that were.

We wrote and wrote. Many of us, like me, ended up with little radio shows and some TV. Andrew advised me never to say no to TV. The people watching in their living rooms were frustrated, and when they heard us communicate what they were thinking, even if we were being ridiculed, they would join us in our fight.

He was right. He was so, so right.

We had a routine. We would rally, and we would learn and plan. We held tutorials on the new media, we attended Republican events (though most of us were fed up with the party), we spoke to thousands of people at rallies all over the country, keeping our narrative simple and straightforward: We wanted to be the voice of the guy who was never heard in the mainstream media. We wanted to be the voice of the patriot.

We always found some cozy pub that smelled like stale beer to gather in after events and conspire. There we would download, celebrate what we had built together, and scheme about our next steps.

The media would continue to mock and defame us, impugning our every move. Andrew would jump on tables for effect to be sure the media took note, and all of us continued to hammer out our message to media: We are coming for you! We *are* you!

By this point, Andrew and I were often on cable news shows back to back, and we had a little texting tradition.

I had the PM drive time show in Birmingham, Alabama. I was still really angry at the establishment, and determined to win. In an effort to state my case with my face, I got a tattoo on my hip bone and I pierced my nose.

Andrew hated it. He never missed a chance to tell me to "pluck that damn thing out of my nose."

But I had my own bone to pick with him. He had grown his hair out and looked like, in my opinion, a street bum. I told him I would remove my nose piercing when he cut his hair. So round and round we would go. The text messages flew back and forth between us. One of the last exchanges took place not long before he died:

Gina: Cut. Your. Hair.
;)
Andrew: Pry that thing out of your nose!
:)
Gina: Lol. Touché.

It was not until that day in March when Andrew Breitbart died that we realized he had been our leader. By the time he died, he had solidified a movement that was bigger than he knew. The whole patriot movement took a collective breath and wondered where we would be without our fearless, happy warrior, Andrew.

I wrote this one, final text to him:

March 1, 2012, 8:53 PM
      Andrew:
      I am compelled to text you one last time to say thank you. God certainly broke the mold when he made you! And you lived more life in your 43 years than most could in 100. I am so glad for that.
      I wrote, recorded and gave interview tributes for you all day, but so much goes unsaid.

As the mom of little ones, my heart especially goes out to your beautiful wife and your family. I know they were your motivation in all you did.

You taught me so much. I know there are thousands or millions out there that you taught, but you taught me that it is okay to risk everything for freedom, and that my enemies are a badge of honor.

I am only emboldened now as I consider our loss of you.

I told you that you needed a haircut. I hope you have taken care of that little matter. You told me I should remove my nose ring. I have.

God bless you and greet you with all the angels today, sweet friend and hero. Oh, how we will celebrate one day!

In Him and in Liberty,

Gina

Your named "Official Troublemaker"—and proud to wear the title! Eph. 3:16–21

How would we go on?

The answer was, like all great leaders, he left us a legacy that continued to guide and inspire us. No one could replace him, but we could all be little parts of him.

Steve Bannon took over Breitbart, and it continued to flourish. I realized, taking stock after the loss of Andrew, that we were everywhere. Our movement, the voice of the little guy, was everywhere. The best part? The establishment still had no idea what was coming. They were busy at their fancy parties, patting themselves on the back and mocking those Tea Party fools. We knew it, and we knew we had them right where we wanted them. They were making the fatal error of underestimating their enemies.

Happy warrioring

From 2012, when Andrew died, until 2015, when Donald J. Trump emerged on the political scene, most of our movement just worked.

Some of us became journalists, some remained opinion leaders, some took to party politics, and others maintained their own voice in their states and towns. We wrote books, we started networks, we were all over social media, and we established a more mature movement that was more effective.

The name "Tea Party" peeled away, and we were mostly just fierce Constitutionalists. In our hearts, we were defined by Andrew Breitbart himself: We were happy warriors.

I left my afternoon drive-time show in my beloved Alabama when my contract was up, because my husband was offered his dream job: fighting the union bosses who were funding the Democrat supermajority machine in California that belonged to Jerry Brown.

Our confidence was high. We had been founders of the Tea Party movement, and we knew how to win. We would take the template that won majorities in both houses of the legislature and the governorship in Missouri, and we would go to California and fight the good fight for the little guy again.

A governor whose party held absolute power was strangling California. But there were more Republicans in California than any other state. If we could expose the corruption and eliminate the fraud, there was hope that the beautiful state of Reagan could be restored to its glory. Like every fight, it would take time.

It wouldn't be easy. We knew that. But I have always said that "as California goes, so goes the country." That meant we had no choice but to save California somehow. We knew the journey would be an adventure, but we had no idea what an epic it would be.

Californication

California is an experiment in socialism. If you like the unprecedented homelessness, debt, and waste of resources, if moral bankruptcy and the abandonment of the rule of law suit you, if you don't mind drugs and trash and sewage on the seashore, then socialism is for you!

California is like the woman who is bum-cluck crazy, doesn't bathe, and engages in constant self-destructive behavior but is so naturally beautiful that she seems worth fighting for. Jerry Brown is like the drug that ruined her. If we could only separate the woman from the evil, she could be herself again.

Living in California is like living the news in full color. I lived right on the beach and could see Tijuana from my front door. I saw illegal immigration as it happened, and Tijuana sewage washed up on our back yard beach. The California government did nothing about it.

Living in California gives you perspective. You *feel* the socialism. I remember the shock I felt waking up to that reality.

Soon after we moved to California, we hosted a birthday party for my little boy on the beach in our backyard. We invited a family from his baseball team over to roast hotdogs and marshmallows on a twelve-inch camper grill behind our house on the vacant beach. (California nights on the beach are almost always cold, so few locals come out.)

Within minutes, two full-size fire trucks pulled up behind us, sirens sounding, lights whirling. We were sure there must be a fire in one of the buildings around us, or a huge bomb threat somewhere nearby. The police were there as well. We soon realized that there was no fire, no emergency—they were there for *us*. I was in disbelief. They told us to put out our fire because four callers had reported us for lighting a fire in our little grill.

I soon learned that cities like West Hollywood actually reward citizens who snitch on their neighbors for burning fires in their own fire places. They give them gift certificates to bars and restaurants for snitching on their neighbors.

The next week, my daughter, with long blonde hair, riding her beach bike (complete with Nantucket-style wicker basket) in white jeans and a polo shirt, was stopped for "looking suspicious." The police said that neighborhood was mostly Mexican, and they wanted to know why she was there. Is that not racial profiling?

It happened again one week later. To this day, she won't drive anything—not a bike, not a car. Thank goodness for all the easy ride apps available today. But their police-state politics scared a little girl for life.

As new residents, my husband and my producer were running errands as we were building a studio. Finding themselves on a dead-end street, they both were checking their navigation on their phones when the police descended and wrote them both tickets for texting while driving. Neither was texting, and they had pulled up to a stop sign. No one was in danger, but the police state has to fund itself somehow.

Much of my commentary on Fox News and in other places over the next couple of years revolved around the unbelievable stories I heard from the immigrants who lived in my neighborhood. Most of my neighbors were longtime residents of our quiet, quirky little beach village, and I came to love them. If I said it once when I saw the latest bicycle concoction invention, or when I learned about the territories divided up by the beach bums and dumpster divers, I must have said these words a million times: "Only in this quirky, little-most-southwesterly beach town!"

Our little beach village was a special place to live. There my children met at the park for the chess club with a few homeless veterans. My daughter volunteered every weekend to make and serve dinner at the local VFW, where class and skin color seemed to matter less to citizens than it did to politicians and police. My blonde children were so often harassed by the police that they all eventually darkened their hair. They told me that unless they were anything but white, they would be constantly harassed.

The most disturbing thing about living there was the stories relayed by the locals. Legal immigrants told us about how they were preyed upon by illegals. Many had lost relatives to drug- or alcohol-induced accidents. Many had lost jobs to illegals, many had been robbed or raped by illegals. Some had opioid-addicted family members, many of them children, who were the drug dealers' clients for life, desperate to get their next high from some of the most addictive substances on earth coming across our southern border. Many begged me to speak for them on television and radio.

The media never mentioned how legal immigrants were hurt by illegal immigration; they made it all about race. Yet in most cases, the victims were the same race as the criminals, and the media and the politicians were often on the side of the criminals.

It gets crazier.

California's environmentalist policies were starving farmers of much-needed fresh water as they flushed billions upon billions of gallons of water out into the ocean to save a few fish. Not a few *species* of fish. Just a few fish. The steelhead trout had been declared endangered by some self-important environmentalists, and twenty-three fish—individual fish—needed a ride to the Pacific. Around five billion gallons of fresh water was released in the first flush, but six fish remained. So, another four billion gallons or so was ordered to be released.

You can't make this stuff up.

Restaurants in California conserve water by making you request water for the table, yet billions of gallons were flowing into the ocean.

Governor Brown decried the evil Republicans and their global warming as he complained that the snow pack will be insufficient to supply the state with fresh water. Then his cronies sent billions of gallons right out into the Pacific.

Farmers were told they were part of the problem and had to live on less water for their crops as Brown and his buddies wasted as much water in one day as the entire Los Angeles metro area would use in a month.

The real crazy had yet to occur.

In 2015, while I was out covering presidential debates around the country, the California legislature passed a bill that would make my husband's work illegal in the state of California. Yes, you read that right. Practically anyone in the world can drive, vote, work, live, collect welfare, and be protected by the constitution in California, except one person: my husband, John.

When he was a state senator in Missouri, John noticed public funds flowing from the union bosses' coffers to Democrat campaigns. Having a perennial lock on taxpayer-funded projects, they had used project labor agreements to ensure that they not only got the jobs without a competitive bid, but also controlled the money flow. Almost all the money then went to elect Democrats to ensure the laws didn't change, and the cycle was self-perpetuating. Until my husband changed all of that.

After his retirement from the senate, he was hired to go to California to audit public projects on behalf of free-market contractors who were getting the shaft under the old corrupt system. Governor Brown, having subsisted on that system for a quarter-century, wasn't going to let John continue working because he was breaking the system and exposing him in the process.

John's work was non-partisan, but the governor planned to shut him down. Ultimately, at Jerry Brown's bidding, two bills were passed (the first one didn't work) to make it illegal for my husband to work in the state of California.

You can imagine our shock. We could not believe that a law could be passed to put one man out of business. But that is exactly what happened. We were gratified when the Pacific Legal Foundation took John's case, planning to fight it all the way to the Supreme Court. They had never lost a case before the Supreme Court, but it would take years for our case to get there, and for now, John couldn't work in California. We had to leave our beloved Golden State and all our friends, and move.

Reasons for seasons

Life changes. Wildly sometimes.

Before we moved from California, I had met Roger Ailes after one of my regular appearances on a Fox Business show. As I was leaving the set, a man approached and told me that Mr. Ailes would like to see me. I was speechless. My assistant, Jason, got a look on his face that told me this man had said what I thought he said. Mr. Ailes, the king of cable television news, wanted to see *me*!

The next several minutes were a blur. I waited in a small room off the main set of C suites. I prayed. I texted my friends to pray. Finally, Mr. Ailes's assistant led me into the inner sanctum. I was sitting face to face with one of the most powerful men in the field I loved.

His presence was huge, and yet shockingly common. His office was cluttered enough to feel comfortable, but not too comfortable to feel informal. He was warm and welcoming, and our visit was like sharing lemonade and cookies with an old friend on a big front porch. I knew that day that my relationship with Mr. Ailes would last for the rest of our lives.

Our conversation was fruitful, and we agreed to meet again and to talk in the meantime. I wanted a job. He wanted a commentator from the border in San Diego where I lived at the time. I asked how I could earn a job at Fox. He said he had a test for me. He wanted me to attend all the 2016 presidential debates and to build a studio, because he didn't like the quality he was getting out of other studios. He wanted me to have the studio built to his specifications, and he gave me people to help with that.

That was the beginning of an amazing series of events that would change the course of my life.

It's…debatable

I had the honor of watching the 2018 Super Bowl with President Trump at his golf club in North Palm Beach, Florida, where I now live, and I took the opportunity to share with him the story of how, during his campaign, I came to trust my own instincts about him. He had won me, and I wanted him to know how…

Like a lot of rides that eventually turn wild, it started in Vegas, the site of the first debate Mr. Ailes asked me to attend and be available for interviews when they needed me. I couldn't decide if I wanted to go. Sixteen candidates would fill the stage, and I would try to get interviews for a national news site I was working with at the time.

As the candidates took the stage, I sat just behind them in a private room for press, next to Chris Matthews, believe it or not. Candidate Trump was new to the crowded primary field, and he wasn't being taken very seriously by many. But I was watching, and my heart had really made my decision when he came down the escalator. But I needed confirmation.

My trusted producer leaned strongly to Trump, and I did too. Two of my most important mentors, Woody and Donna Woodrum, personally knew many of the Trumps and had spoken highly of them for years. They would be heading up California for Trump. And my political mentors in media seemed to be leaning that way too. But there were so many logical reasons I needed to keep quiet in my support of him.

It would have been so much easier for me to stay in lock-step with my friends and my husband's company than to go on TV and work against them. I knew there would be fallout from a decision like that. The board of my husband's company had already voted to contribute to another candidate, and my friends were all on board with Cruz. I had initially said yes to co-chairing Women for Cruz California, and Donald Trump was the only candidate I didn't know at all.

But I liked Trump's plain-spokenness. I liked his relatability. And I liked his passion to fix the illegal immigration problem that plagued my little town and all the hard-working legal immigrants there—a problem all the other candidates were ducking.

Trump did a good job at the debate. A darn good job, and he was treated terribly by the other candidates and the press. What was it that they hated about him? I was pleasantly surprised by much of what he was saying, and I wanted to know more.

After the debate, I watched as the candidates filed into the press gaggle where I was strategically positioned. They made straight for the "alphabet soup" media—ABC, NBC, CBS, and the rest. Then, in true form, they disappeared. Hundreds of citizen journalists, bloggers, and smaller news networks stood dejected, undoubtedly wondering if it was even worth it to have traveled all the way to Las Vegas.

My candidate until the now famous "escalator moment" when Donald Trump announced for president of the United States, Ted Cruz, was one of the first to duck out of the follow up press gaggle. After I had interviewed him many times, raised money for him, and even agreed to work for him in California, he now barely gave me the time of day. But that was how he and all the other candidates acted as well that day. It was clear they thought they didn't need us, which hurt and annoyed me.

Then I noticed that one candidate had not abandoned the gaggle. Donald Trump was still there, shaking hands and giving interviews, and the press was all over him because he was the only one remaining. I watched this reality-show-star-turned-presidential-candidate work the crowd. His energy seemed boundless. His heart seemed open. He had earned his place on the stage that night.

He stayed for a long time, and I watched as every single outlet, big or small, had an audience with the future president, including me.

Before that debate, many in the press, including me, did not take Trump seriously. But that evening changed my view. As a founding member of the Tea Party movement, I had prayed for someone to disrupt the status quo. Now I believed this man would win.

I had never seen any national candidate for any office stay until the last unknown blogger was gone, but that is exactly what I watched that night. Five hundred reporters dwindled to one hundred, then seventy-five, then twenty, then five—and Donald Trump stayed. I didn't know much about this candidate yet, but I knew one thing: He cared about even the least powerful in media. What did that suggest about his willingness to listen to the little guy on Main Street?

Time would answer that for me in full color!

New York

Soon after the press gaggle moment, I was in New York doing my normal network hits, and I was invited to a dinner with Corey Lewan-dowski, Hope Hicks, Sean Hannity, Kimberly Guilfoyle, Bill Shine, and a small cadre of others.

I was deep in thought as we walked from the News Corp building to Ruth's Chris Steakhouse a few blocks away. I was shocked that no one bothered Sean Hannity, who just walked the streets like any common person. And Kimberly Guilfoyle somehow made the trek in Louboutins.

Anyone who has ever worn Louboutins knows they are barely tolerable for quick photo ops, let alone for blocks of walking. My mind was fixating on these little wonders as I knew I had an important decision to make very soon. This would be my chance to gather enough information to decide what the next many months of my life would be.

Sitting between Hope and Corey, I asked as many questions as they would answer about this interesting candidate Donald Trump. What would his policy on Iran look like? Was he an isolationist? Why did he ever support Democrats? My list went on.

Inquisitive by nature, I concentrated hard and listened intently. An hour into the evening, I realized I was probably waxing wonky, and who wants *that* guy at dinner? I tried to lighten up. A glass of wine became my vehicle to pretend that the pressure I felt in that moment to gather data didn't weigh on my shoulders as much as it did. I understand why Jesus included wine with fellowship. I needed to engage, not do research.

After some laughs and some fun, Hope turned to me with a serious look, and the gravity of her glare made my heart race. "Would you be willing to be a media surrogate for Mr. Trump?" she asked me plainly.

I felt all the pressure of the evening mount in my face in that moment, and I covered my mouth with my napkin, wishing I could hide behind it.

I couldn't answer her yet. I worried that my integrity as an analyst might be compromised if I climbed aboard with this man I didn't know so soon after jumping off the Cruz ship. But in time I realized I was too fed up with the insanity of a party that always supported candidates who couldn't win. In my gut, I believed that Donald J. Trump could win, and I accepted Hope's invitation to become a campaign surrogate for my candidate. I lost friends, business partners, and money because of the choice I made that night, but it was the best political decision I ever made.

PART TWO

THE PROBLEM WITH CRAZY

CHAPTER 5

THE POLITICS OF ANGER

How the Left Attacks the Messenger and Blames the Victim

"Political language...is designed to make lies sound truthful and murder respectable, and to give an appearance of solidity to pure wind."
　　　　　　　　—George Orwell[1]

"When you resort to attacking the messenger and not the message, you have lost the debate."
　　　　　　　　—Addison Whithecomb[2]

"Political tags—such as royalist, communist, democrat, populist, fascist, liberal, conservative, and so forth—are never basic criteria. The human race divides politically into those who want people to be controlled and those who have no such desire."
　　　　　　　　—Robert A. Heinlein[3]

The bubble

The government and media elite dwell in a bubble, feeding on three things: power, money, and fame. For decades, the bubble-dwellers took it for granted that these were the only things that mattered. They were understood. They were accepted. They were nurtured. They were protected.

Then a billionaire builder flowed down an escalator with his super-model immigrant wife who speaks five languages, and the bubble began to quiver with anxiety. They could hope he was an idiot, but that was unlikely, given his Wharton degree. It was even more unlikely when you considered that Donald Trump built buildings and had projects all over the United States and the world that others said were impossible. But if he wasn't stupid, could he be crazy?

Could a crazy person break through all the predictions about his presidency? They said he would never run. He did. They said his support would never break 20 percent. It did. They said he would bomb in the first debate, and then in the second, and so on. His popularity only grew. So if they couldn't prove he was crazy, what could the frantic establishment throw at him that would stick?

He was mean.

The media spent weeks spinning a tale about Trump mocking a handicapped reporter. But the gesture Trump used to mock the reporter turned out to be the same gesture he used when talking about many people who didn't understand something he said. It was all on tape. There was nothing there. So now what?

The frantic elite were desperate to shut him down. He had to go. If he burst the bubble of their power, they would all be in free fall, and the landing would be hard. They could all lose their jobs. They could have to work harder and longer to earn the same money if the bureaucracy was not there to coddle them. This sounded like a fate worse than death to many, and they were ready to fight to the death for their precious bubble.

The good news for the bubble elite was that there were so many of them: the lobbyists who work in cahoots with the consultants, the Hollywood elite who are their donors, the politicians, their staffs, Wall Street and the business elite who loved their tax favors, and the media. They were willing to stop at nothing, the tactical advantages were all on their side.

A spherical war

The elite saw Trump as a wrecking ball. No one had ever legitimately threatened them. This was war. At first, they figured they could bully him. But when bullying came back to bite them, they realized they might be in trouble.

Prior to Trump, they could bully and buy off politicians. Politicians need money and media to be elected, but this billionaire builder didn't need their money or their media. In fact, he got more earned media with a single tweet than all their lobbyists could buy! He got headlines when he went to dinner or bought a tie. How could consultants control him?

They couldn't. So they began a campaign of hate and anger the likes of which we had never seen before.

The rules of engagement in the war of personal power maintenance

"Nice guys finish last," said Leo Durocher. And Saul Alinsky added, "Last guys don't finish nice."

As Barack Obama knew, Saul Alinsky is the king of community disruption in our age. Every union, every resistance disrupter, and every Soros protester knows Alinsky's rules and how to employ them.

Andrew Breitbart taught me about Alinsky in one of our very first meetings over dinner, with a small group of other early Tea Party founders. He warned me that a revolution would be bloody, because the radicals have all read *Rules for Radicals*. He warned me that they would accuse me of the things they were actually doing.

He was wrong about the bloody revolution, by the mercy of God, and the wisdom of our Founding Fathers. He was right about the daily isolation and name calling.

If they were astroturfing, they would accuse us of astroturfing. If they were radicals, they would call us radicals. If they were racists, they would accuse us of racism. It was sometime around that time when I admonished Siri to start calling me the "racist homophobic sexist bigot"—all the things I am not—just so I'd be immune to it every day when others said it about me.

Manufactured outrage

"The first step in community organization is community disorganization," wrote Alinsky. "The organizer must first rub raw the resentments of the people in the community..."

If the instigators don't have a critical mass of angry people, they don't have any power. So they must continually enrage their base, keeping them "raw." To keep them raw, they have to continually agitate. Every shooting has to be about the guns. Every terrorist attack has to be about disadvantaged refugees. Every economic downturn has to be about rich people preying on poor people, about men being paid more than women, and about white people intentionally keeping black people down.

That is the strategy behind the division and identity politics with which the left energizes its supporters and drives them to the voting booth.

The outrageous thing is that perpetual identity politics is itself racist. No one denies that America's heart is scarred by the sins of the past, including slavery. But the left must exploit that in order to control its base and extract votes.

While they scream about the right being "racist," you need only look at any city controlled exclusively by leftists—Chicago, Detroit, St. Louis...—to see that they are the ones who keep people down.

Plantation politics

Obviously, there is no greater scar on the heart of America than that we committed against ourselves...that of slavery. Thank God for the strong leadership that ended the horrific injustice, and for those who have made sure we never re-visit that low. I don't believe we ever will.

However, great civilizations throughout history have fallen due to socialist tyranny, and I can't help but be confounded by how much freedom some will trade for free stuff.

I call it "plantation politics." Its victims, poor and abused, suffer from higher rates of illness, infant mortality, suicide, substance abuse, and fatal accidents, and they die younger than the rest of the population. Families on the modern-day plantation have been torn apart by policies that encourage unwed motherhood and discourage fathers from sticking around and by a culture of sexual license that has particularly punishing consequences for the poor.

The murder of the plantation's children by abortion is well funded: almost $1.5 million in taxpayer money is funneled to Planned Parenthood *every single day*.[4] Most of Planned Parenthood's abortion clinics are in leftist strongholds, where they target minorities.[5]

The money Planned Parenthood raises is turned right around to fund Democrat election campaigns. Based on 2016 data released by the Federal Election Commission, Planned Parenthood's political action committee contributed 98% of their funds to Democrat politicians.[6] Everybody gets rich—Planned Parenthood executives, Democrat politicians, and the doctors who kill the minority babies. Who is hurt? Only the women and children stuck on the plantation and America's taxpayers.

Sadly, most of this system's victims don't appreciate their own plight. On the plantations of the 1850s, slaves at least knew they were enslaved. Murder was called murder, and slavery was called slavery. Today they box it up in pretty, palatable packages and call it "welfare," "social justice," and "women's health services."

I'm not saying that all Democrats or even all leftists would ever endorse slavery. I truly believe most don't even see the damage done by their policies, or they wouldn't support them. But how much oppression is tolerable? The problem with regressive socialism has always been that it only thrives in oppression. Oppression of some sort is a necessary byproduct of socialism, which is why socialism has essentially destroyed every culture that has tried it.

I believe that black people and other minorities are slowly getting wise to what is happening to their communities. Black people voted for Donald Trump in record numbers, despite the left's relentless attempts to smear him as a racist. And after only one year as president, Donald Trump ushered in an economic climate that allowed record high homeownership among blacks, and record low unemployment.

There is something in the human psyche that yearns to be free. This is why revolutions happen. Eventually, the enslaved begin to see the light, and they take steps to overthrow their oppressors.

Donald Trump received more black votes than both Romney and McCain. The leftist elite know they must prepare for this awakening; so they are recruiting. And they are doing it under the guise of "compassion."

They promote Sanctuary Cities because, they say, they care about wayward illegal immigrants. Of course they care! They care about building another poor, dependent voting block to assure they keep their power and money, because not enough actual Americans will vote for them anymore.

They say they want to house refugees. But the reality is that most refugees would rather stay in their homeland. The United States is the major funder of temporary safe housing for refugees close to their own homes and out of harm's way. Most refugees would rather stay in these safe zones until they can return to their homes. But refugees who stay home don't become useful voters in America.

The left's identity politics may be running out of steam, however. On November 11, 2016, the *Washington Post* declared, "Identity politics failed to clinch a Clinton win." Latinos were a full six points short of what polls predicted. Human Rights Watch reported that identity politics is not only failing in America, but that it is failing globally. The president's popularity has been gradually climbing with all minorities, especially Hispanics, since his election.

If that is all true, then Democrat elites have to keep working to fund their machine. They must recruit other denizens and convince them they are victims, that their enemy is the right, and that free stuff (social programs) is freedom.

The true racists are those willing to "rub raw the resentments" of an entire community to serve their own lust for power and money. Real racism is the willingness to prey on those most vulnerable. If the regressive, socialist left succeeds in bringing down America, history proves that the most vulnerable will suffer most. If there is no America to protect freedom, then the young, the infirm, the elderly, and minorities become the first victims of totalitarianism.

When my cousin (we don't really know this, but we enjoy the possible connection), New Zealander Trevor Loudon wrote his first book on communists hiding within our own government, he was dismissed as a conspiracy nut. People looked at us as if we were crazy when we held a small book-signing party for him at a cafe in Birmingham, Alabama, where I had a radio talk show at the time. Now we know that he was absolutely right. His carefully compiled data on our own politicians proved they were working to overthrow American constitutional governance in favor of socialism.

Trevor stayed at our home in Alabama. My children liked to call him "cousin" Trevor, and they loved his melodic accent and quirky passion for America. One night at dinner, my daughter Lyda asked him why he cares so much about what happens in America when he lives in New Zealand.

His answer was swift and sure: "Because, dear Lyda, as America goes, so goes the rest of the world."

My husband replied by quoting his favorite president, Ronald Reagan, who in his "Shining City on a Hill" speech warned, "Freedom is never more than one generation away from extinction. We didn't pass it to our children in the bloodstream. It must be fought for, protected, and handed on for them to do the same."

The soft underbelly of the left

"History repeats itself, first as tragedy, second as farce."
—Karl Marx[7]

The goal of the socialist, regressive left is to dismantle all that is American.

That's why you will rarely find them criticizing those who burn flags, who hate America, or who rewrite history. Some on the left even consider breaking a law, burning a flag, or refusing to fight in a war "patriotic."

If America remembers who she is, good and bad, that undermines the objective of the left to disrupt and rub raw, as Alinsky, Trotsky, Lenin, Marx, Stalin, and their other mentors instructed.

But aside from their problem of the enslaved catching on to their dirty scheme, they face a more present dilemma. The left has long fooled the grassroots into thinking they are acting out of compassion, while collecting big money from the elite. Wall Street, for example, donates far more to the Democrat politicians than they do to the Republicans. But you would never know that when you listen to their campaign to pit the poor against the rich.

Blaming the rich for all of the problems of the poor while collecting big checks from the rich has worked well for the Democrat elite. The limousine liberal can assuage his guilt by writing checks to Democratic politicians to keep the poor at bay, getting nights in the Lincoln Bedroom, and invitations to all the right parties in return.

President Trump succinctly and aptly called this system the "swamp." And as I have said on Fox News, the swamp isn't going to drain itself.

When I worked as press secretary in my husband's senate office in Missouri, I learned secrets no politician wants you to know. I learned a lot that I didn't want to know, but if I didn't know it, I couldn't understand the vitriol directed at the president as clearly as I do.

A little story about politics

The system works like this: The Rich Guy in Hollywood or on Wall Street writes a big check to leftist Swamp Politician. Swamp Politician passes legislation that doesn't matter to anyone except the elite, like tax loopholes for the very rich or transgender bathrooms. Rich Guy feels good because his guilt over being so rich has been relieved without ever having to look Poor Person in the eye to help him.

Low Life Lobbyist collects big money from Rich Guy and gives it to Swamp Politician too. Then Low Life Lobbyist has access to both Swamp Politician and Rich Guy. This means he can use Rich Guy's money to take Swamp Politician and his friends to fancy dinners in D.C., and *he* gets to decide who gets elected next, because after all, Low Life Lobbyist controls the purse strings of Rich Guy.

Once Low Life Lobbyist has leveraged checks from Rich Guy for New Politician to be elected, New Politician is the puppet of the three—Low Life Lobbyist, Swamp Politician, and Rich Guy, the last of whom is the source of all the money. Now the trio controls yet another lawmaker, and has even more control over the enslaved Poor Person—who, clueless that he is being used, continues to vote for those controlling him.

At this point, as momentum builds and the swamp cycle continues, that same trio—Low Life Lobbyist, the conduit to Swamp Politician and Rich Guy—gets to choose the staffs, make the appointments, draft the legislation, and even choose the parking places (this is a bigger deal than you think) for all the Swamp Politicians. They do it all on the back of Poor Person, and all they have to do to keep their power, money, and fame is continue recruiting Poor People, and keep them poor by convincing them they are victims, willing to trade freedoms for free stuffs.

All of this works beautifully for the proprietors of the plantation and the swamp monsters until someone shines a little light on the system, and the people decide to drain the swamp.

The Tea Party recognized the role of the establishment Republicans and Democrats in this swamp cycle. Leftists want to disrupt and overthrow constitutional governance, and there are GOP officeholders who are willing to compromise and look the other direction in the name of "statesmanship" so that Low Life Lobbyist and Rich Guy will help him get re-elected.

The Tea Party, therefore, called out not only the leftists seeking to destroy the republic, but also those on the right who looked the other way—the GOP establishment. Complicity is still corruption.

Donald Trump came to the swamp with a hook to pull the drain plug. From that moment, he became the target of all the above-mentioned players, who depend on the swamp apparatus to keep their fame, fortune, and power.

At first, they didn't believe he was serious. After all, he had played the game. He had given money to all of them to get his businesses permitted, because he was committed to his companies when that was his job.

But at some point, Donald Trump wanted more. It wasn't more money, or more fame, or more power. He was king of his own castle. He was surrounded by yes-men who told him how shiny his buildings were and how smart he was every day. He needed nothing. And there is nothing more dangerous to swamp monsters than someone who doesn't need Rich Guy, Low Life Lobbyist, or Swamp Politician and his friends.

Donald J. Trump was an existential threat to the establishment, both Republican and Democrat. He was a nuclear bomb. Worse, he knew their system and how to dismantle it. And he needed nothing from them. He was lethal to everything they held sacred. He was not only a threat to their wealth and fame and power, but to their entire sense of importance. Without their job inside the bureaucratic bubble, they feel like—and are—nothing.

When the lies have run dry, where will they go? Now that President Trump and the conservative crusaders have exposed their underbelly, they fear the gig is up. They could not only lose everything they dreamed of, they could be exposed for being the corrupt liars they are. Therefore, they must fight.

But there is a problem. There is a big problem, and the bubble has absolutely no idea what to do about it.

The commie-care conflict

Why are the left so adamant about political correctness? Why are they so concerned if someone is "offended"? When someone disagrees with them, they are willing to unfriend him or her on social media and even remove family and friends from their lives.

They usurp the symbols of conservatism, like the rainbow; they steal the words of conservatives, like "tolerance"; and they even steal the ideals of conservatives, like "freedom." And they turn them into something they are not. Why?

It is because they want to make only certain thought lines acceptable. "The smart way to keep people passive and obedient is to strictly limit the spectrum of acceptable opinion, but allow very lively debate within that spectrum," wrote the radical academic Noam Chomsky.[8] For example, you can think in terms of tolerance, but there is no tolerance for Christianity, conservatism, or Western culture. That is just the beginning of their limit on acceptable opinions.

Leftists advocate for feminism, but some of them stop at criticizing Islamic oppression, like female genital mutilation, child marriage, or stoning women to death. Why? Is it because they can import Muslims and use them for their votes? Muslims also help in the disruption they want to create in Western culture.

Most importantly, Muslims are reproducing faster than any other racial group (about 2.9 children per Muslim couple), which means votes and power in the future. So the leftist elites limit the discussion. If politically necessary, they will overlook the very women's rights they defend in public. So much for feminism. Instead of having a real conversation about Sharia law and feminism, they march their largely unsuspecting people through the streets in pink "pussy" hats reminiscent of dunce caps. Most don't realize that they aren't even fighting for all women, or that they are being used to further a narrative that leaves certain women behind, like Muslim women.

Leftists talk a lot about gay rights, but they overlook the brutal treatment of gays in Islamic cultures. Homosexuality is punished by death under Sharia. But instead of talking about that, the left limits the conversation to bathrooms and wedding cakes.

The left loves to get uninformed Americans to cry "victim" and act as if removing monuments to slave owners or Confederate soldiers will remove that scar on American history. It won't. So why do they do this? They are following Alinksy's advice to "rub raw" the sensitivities and foment disorder to divide and undermine America so they can overthrow it. Some believe that there are those on the left who do not care if America is dead if they are the undertakers.

Socialists love disorder, and Islamic Sharia Law is a partner in the left's desire to topple Western civilization. That's why so many are silent on Islamic terror and the peril of Sharia Law. If Democrats were consistent in their compassion for children or their disdain for monuments to oppressors, then why do they tolerate the veneration of Mohammad, a slave owner and child-abuser? It's because they see Islam as a partner in the overthrow of an America they resent. What other reason would there be?

Socialists love their unions. Well, not really. But they find them very useful—especially the union bosses. The bosses work like wealthy CEOs, reaping the benefits of workers' mandatory dues while trying to convince the rank and file that they have it good. It isn't surprising that when you look a little deeper, the left never says a word when jobs go overseas because the unions are charging too much for products or services. No one who sees the elite for what they are is shocked that the union bosses never fight against illegal immigration, even though they know that the illegals are taking their members' jobs. It was never about the members, anyway. The unions are largely a Democrat funding machine that uses its members for their dues.

Leftists talk a lot about how savage Christianity is and about the separation of church and state (a phrase that is nowhere in the U.S. Constitution). Yet they look the other way when "pastors" like Jesse Jackson want to preach and make millions for their political activities. They also say that politics from the pulpit is all wrong. But Jesse Jackson makes his living from Operation PUSH, a political church I have visited in the city of Chicago. He preaches politics every day, in and out of the pulpit; but since it is leftist politics, the left is quiet. As long as he delivers Democrat voters, and keeps the elite in power, he can blend church and state all he wants.

Leftists say climate change is the most important issue of our time. But they are quiet when Al Gore travels the globe in a jet with a giant carbon footprint. In the regressive leftist world, you aren't allowed to criticize Al Gore or any other liberal. They're immune to their own rules.

Leftists say they care about poverty. But you won't hear them talk about Bernie Sanders's multiple homes or his car collection that would make Jay Leno blush.

Leftists say they care about Mexicans. But it is common knowledge that many illegals are raped or killed trying to come over the border from Mexico, and the left is silent. Why? And if they truly care about immigrants at all, then they would care that most crime exacted on Americans by illegals happens to legal immigrants. But again, silence from the left.

Leftists say they care about "Dreamers" (DACA recipients). But they rejected an offer by the president to give them a path to citizenship in exchange for a wall to secure that same citizenship.

Leftists say they will fight for families separated by ICE agents at the Mexican border. But if they have their way and ICE is abolished, gangs will prey on legal immigrant communities, human trafficking will flourish, and worse, every foreigner who wants to get into America for free will simply kidnap a child, say he's its parent, and walk across the border to be set free to harm and violate that child in any way he pleases, no questions asked. "Families" are separated only to determine that they actually related, and to prevent the rape and kidnapping of children. And yet the left is protesting this protection.

Leftists say they care about black people, but what about the prenatal genocide that Planned Parenthood conducts disproportionately against black babies with taxpayer funds? What about the mass murders every single weekend in the black neighborhoods of Chicago?

All this confounds conservatives, who see the hypocrisy but can't imagine why you can't even say certain words or make certain logical arguments any more. It isn't for the reasons leftists claim. It isn't because you are racist or sexist or homophobic or bigoted. It's because *they* are.

They must stop you from thinking critically, or their hypocrisy and political agenda will be destroyed.

Oh so delightfully useful

"The useful idiots, the leftists who are idealistically believing in the beauty of the Soviet socialist or Communist or whatever system, when they get disillusioned, they become the worst enemies. That's why my KGB instructors specifically made the point: never bother with leftists. Forget about these political prostitutes. Aim higher. [...] They serve a purpose only at the stage of destabilization of a nation. For example, your leftists in the United States: all these professors and all these beautiful civil rights defenders. They are instrumental in the process of the subversion only to destabilize a nation. When their job is completed, they are not needed any more. They know too much. Some of them, when they get disillusioned, when they see that Marxist-Leninists come to power—obviously they get offended—they think that they will come to power. That will never happen, of course. They will be lined up against the wall and shot."

—Tomas Schuman[9]

The money that moves the socialist political machine is the big, big money. It's the Hollywood elite, the George Soroses of the world, and even the wealthiest Wall Street CEOs. But that secret can never get to their useful idiots, or they risk losing everything.

But here is the problem: They need the votes of Joe Six Pack, who detests Hollywood, Wall Street, and billionaires like Soros. They can't let him know that is where they get their money.

Unlike Republicans, who are mostly middle-class Americans, Democrat politicians often can't fundraise very well off of their base. They have to keep much of their base poor, dependent, and believing their politicians will save them. So they have no choice but to fundraise from billionaires in exchange for control. Together, they distort the narrative, they disorganize the culture, and they outlaw certain words, phrases, ideas, and even historical facts. They lie and manipulate to maintain their wealth and control, using the useful wherever they can. And usually, the useful idiots are unaware.

But they have another problem.

Ideologically, Joe Six Pack votes for the socialists only because he still remembers them as the party of the little guy. He votes for his union because he believes his union gets benefits for him that he wouldn't otherwise have. He votes for the party of Kennedy, even though today John F. Kennedy's views on abortion, gun control, and marriage would make him anathema in the Democrat Party.

Joe Six Pack woke up one day and realized that his party had abandoned him. Without him, the Democrat politicians have few votes. But without Soros, Wall Street, and Hollywood, the doesn't have enough money. So then what?

That is the crossroads where the Democrat Party finds itself today.

They lied to their base, and their base knows it. Joe Six Pack sees record-breaking economic success; he sees millions of new jobs; he sees open pipelines that Democrats won't open, just to please the environmentalists; he sees manufacturing thriving in the rust belt; he sees reduced crime in inner cities after decades of Democrat rule and decay; he sees regulation cuts enabling a thriving job market and record-low unemployment; and he sees high consumer confidence and reduced debt. Joe Six Pack sees the America he remembers.

He has been seeing it for a while.

Prior to President Trump, I didn't even want to call myself a Republican or a Democrat, but a lot has changed under his leadership. Part of draining the swamp for President Trump meant flushing establishment Republicans and Democrats and leaving the people in control. That is another reason he has been so harshly criticized and attacked, leaving the Democratic Party in shambles. There isn't much left once their elite are exposed.

Under Obama, the Democrats lost more than a thousand seats at the state and local levels.

Trump won by more votes than any Republican nominee in history.

Trump won record numbers with blacks and Hispanics.

In the first hundred days of the Trump presidency, while the media screamed about the flailing president, the GOP won five special elections, including the single most expensive one in the Democrats' history, in which the Democrat National Committee spent $30 million dollars and lost.

DNC fundraising was flat, while the new, Trumpian GOP outraised them three-to-one. Most of the GOP money came in small donations. That meant Joe Six Pack sent money to the GOP and the grassroots approved of the president. That meant the media were still using the same fake polls they used during the campaign—and the same fake narrative—and middle America wasn't buying it.

During the campaign, they called Trump a racist and a misogynist, and when that didn't work, they pulled "anti-Semite" out of their bag of tricks. With a Jewish daughter and grandchildren, that didn't work so well. Nancy Pelosi, the minority leader in Congress called President Trump "anti-immigrant." That would be hard to prove since he is married to one.

Nothing stuck, so then the media just complained that Trump was Teflon.

Maybe he was Teflon. Maybe their attacks were just pathetic and dishonest, and the American people could see right through them.

Then Trump committed the sin of sins: He won.

The left demanded a recount of the presidential election. That didn't work.

They latched on to their Russian conspiracy theory. That didn't work either.

Next, Soros funded the phony "Resist" movement, then little sub-movements popped up and fell. But those who were supposed to be protesting were more comfortable eating cheetos in bed in their mama's basements. Fail. Utter flop.

A New Democrat?

The Democrats decided they must be losing with their base because they didn't have the right slogan, so they regrouped and came up with a new one! Someone brilliant invented the mantra "A better deal," hoping to grab *Make America Great Again* by the throat and win. But they didn't. And they won't. Because it isn't possible, as long as America is awake. But in their arrogance, they haven't accepted that.

They used the death of a woman at a National Socialist vs. Antifa confrontation in Charlottesville to try to resuscitate their "Trump-is-a-racist" narrative, which failed during the campaign. They took to the airwaves to scream "white supremacy" and tried once again to link President Trump, his voters, and the small balanced media to the KKK. It backfired.

The left needs both the amoral elite and the moral grassroots. But you can't have both. The more you mix the two, the closer you are to death.

When it became apparent they were losing, they only screamed louder. Large media made massive layoffs. Leftist media fired people, laid them off, and got on TV with crinkled faces in response to the smell of their own failure. One by one, former heroes of the dying establishment elite faded off into the sunset...and America shut the door behind them.

America was ready for the winning that President Trump promised. America was ready to find herself again, to rediscover Reagan's shining city on a hill. America was ready to be that place where life, liberty, and the pursuit of happiness are realities again. America was ready to be great again.

The difference

"Look closer; see ME!"
—Anonymous

The left must convince the public that they are compassionate so they can be the giver of all free stuff, making more dependents who will vote for them. It doesn't look so bad on its face...that is, until you look closer.

The main difference between conservatives and the left regarding charity is that the left needs to divide people into groups and convince them they are victims. Then the government can provide for them, and the elite can maintain their power. It's Orwellian.

Conservatives want small government because they understand that it is actually far more compassionate. Instead of government "caring" for those less fortunate, friends, family, churches, and neighbors do.

This accomplishes two good things:

The giver has to look the needy person in the eye. There is a level of compassion there that a government will never give. There is a human touch there, a glance of empathy, a smile, a tear, a prayer...government is capable of none of this.

And the needy person has to look the giver back in the eye. This provides a level of accountability for what is given. This can motivate the needy person to try harder to pull himself up. That's better for the needy person and better for the giver, who gets to witness the fruits of his labor and the victory of overcoming!

Thus, the standoff.

The leftist cannot accept personal responsibility, because to do so would destroy the very political structure on which he depends for his own power and money. The conservative cannot accept government provision for the needy, because he has a moral conflict with the system that makes people dependent, uses them only for votes, and never really looks them in the eye.

The left is paranoid to the point of delusion, because they know they live in a house of cards. The right is frustrated because they are called names and labeled when they are simply trying to speak the truth and help people.

One side talks, and the other side acts. One side sees victims, and the other side sees victors. One side talks about death, and the other side talks about life.

Astute observers see this when they carefully examine the facts alone, and are honest and courageous enough to acknowledge the truth they see.

I am sad for those who have been abandoned by a party that no longer seems to care about the rank and file members. I love competition, and I believe a better Democratic Party would make a better Republican Party. I want both parties accountable to their members, committed to the battle of ideas and in a constant state of funneling power from the elites, elected, media, and money down to the people who vote. That is my dream for the two parties of America. I believe that most of my Democrat friends want the same thing. We would all be better for that. Without that, one party will die, and the American system will correct itself without it.

CHAPTER 6

WAR ON THE HEARTLAND

How the Left Attacks the Messenger and Blames the Victim

"California's a wonderful place to live—if you happen to be an orange."
—Fred Allen[1]

"It's a scientific fact that if you stay in California you lose one point of your IQ every year."
—Truman Capote[2]

If you want to kill something quickly, you stab it in the heart.

We have watched as the left stabs the heart of America over and over again. One commentator on a chat thread, speaking for middle America and the Rust Belt, wrote, "The modern left finds it more virtuous to hire a wealthy black man or a wealthy white woman than to hire a poor, white man. Rural America knows."

I won't even comment on tolerance or equality here, but it seems our compassion is way off, doesn't it? The left has vilified whole segments of society regions of the country. I hate to say it, but I believe the left-wing elite want to kill our country, at least as we know it. I believe they want power and money over anything else, and they are willing to let the whole country be a graveyard as long as they are the undertakers.

That accusation may make conservatives uncomfortable. We are called "haters" so often that we are reluctant to make that accusation, even when it's deserved.

But think about it. It wouldn't be unusual for power-hungry elitists to accept the death of a country so they could control it. That's been the story of every country that has fallen throughout history. We know it is at least possible that the elite care more about power for themselves than freedom for those who gave them power.

I am originally from Missouri, in the heartland of the United States. I grew up along the shores of the muddy Mississippi, summering at the Lake of the Ozarks, and enjoying a culture rich with history and patriotism.

The Lake of the Ozarks is still my favorite place in the whole world. The Ozarks are special. The mountains fall right into the lake, which, with its winding coves, has more coastline than Lake Michigan. Life is simple there. We learned how to make our own fun and adventure, celebrating that special beauty we somehow knew was a best kept secret just for us.

The grass is a deep, lush, green-blue on the mountains. One of my favorite novels was written in those mountains. *Shepherd of the Hills* by Harold Bell Wright was an instant classic, and for decades its sales were second only to the Holy Bible.

There is a reason Mr. Bell left his home in New York and traveled all the way to Branson, Missouri, in 1898 to write his novel. His doctor had advised him to go for health reasons, but I believe he went to immerse himself in the American values that are so powerful in the heart of the country. There he met John and Anna Ross, who were known locally as Old Matt and Aunt Mollie. They became the centerpiece of his classic novel.

Those of us who know the green grassy hills and curvy-shored lakes of the Ozarks understand why this is called the heartland. It is here that the critical blood supply of all that is American is pumped to the rest of the nation. Here is the essential organ to the body of America and the world.

Every country song I hear reminds me of my home state of Missouri and the heartland. I wrote my doctoral dissertation on love in the heartland and the experience of extraordinary love. What makes love last? What makes love come? What makes love, this intangible force, so important to us that people live for it and die for it every day?

And as I watch the politics unfold and the attacks from the coasts on the heartland, I think I can see why their attacks on the heartland might be more intentional than is apparent at first blush.

The heartland expands beyond Missouri and even the Midwest.

Kid Rock's song "All Summer Long," one of my favorites, is about Lake Michigan, but I believe it captures the feeling of growing up on the shores of the Lake of the Ozarks:

> We were tryin' different things and we were smokin' funny
>   things,
> Makin' love out by the lake to our favorite song.
> Sippin' whiskey out the bottle, not thinkin' 'bout tomorrow,
> Singin' Sweet Home Alabama, all summer long!

I never tried smoking anything funny except straw once, out of curiosity (better than eating Tide Pods like millennials do these days!). I was pretty straight-laced, a typical Midwestern girl, and I didn't want to disappoint my mom. I still relate to the culture as depicted in this song, and we sure did sing "Sweet Home Alabama" all the time. It came as no surprise, then, that as soon as my broadcast career launched, I found myself moving to the flagship radio station for my company in Birmingham, Alabama. That is where my career began to take off, and I found my footing in the complexities of my dreams.

I can tell you, the heartland pumps out essential blood supply from the South, too. I fell head over heels in love with Alabama, and my audience there is still deeply knitted in my heart! Alabama will always be my "sweet home" in my mind, and I always say that the right job offer would have me right back in Alabama yelling "Roll Tide" every season!

But from there I spent five years in California, and much of my work life in New York and Washington, D.C., and I can tell you that these are the extremities of our nation. Wisdom abounds on the coasts, but not the kind of wisdom that comes from living in the heartland or the South. Like a body, the extremities are nothing without their vital organs, and they have a type of peripheral neurosis. The coasts are lacking blood supply from the main organs; they are numb, distorted, disoriented. They cannot survive without the heartland. But they don't know that. Those who want the whole body of America to die have convinced the extremities that they not only can survive without the heartland and vital organs, but should shed them.

I have noticed, in particular, three indications of the left's attempt to end America. They aren't the only such indications, but they are illuminating. Watch for these to emerge if the socialists on the left continue to take control of one party.

The Electoral College argument

When President Trump was elected, there was immediate outrage by coastal elites who complained he didn't win the popular vote. "If it weren't for those idiots in the heartland, it wouldn't have happened. Trump would not be president." That's what many of them thought.

Suddenly the Electoral College was a target of leftist ire. "I think it needs to be eliminated. I'd like to see us move beyond it," said Hillary Clinton. "The Electoral College was meant to stop men like Trump from being President," opined *The Atlantic* on November 21, 2016.

The Electoral College is a not a place or even an institution. It's a *process* that our Founding Fathers established in the U.S. Constitution as a sort of compromise between letting the states' representatives in Congress elect a president and electing the president through a national popular vote. The Founders knew that the latter kind of election had proved to be a threat to republics throughout history.

The president of the United States is elected by a majority of the 538 electors appointed by the states. Article II of the Constitution provides:

"Each state shall appoint, in such manner as the legislature thereof may direct, a number of electors, equal to the whole number of senators and representatives to which the state may be entitled in the Congress." Missouri, for example, currently has eight U.S. representatives and, like every state, two senators, so it has ten electors.

While many call for its abolition, some understand that the Electoral College provides stability and ensures that areas of the country like the heartland—areas that don't have a massive population or financial centers—still count in a presidential election.

If the Electoral College were eliminated, the financial and population centers would most certainly control elections. That means wealthy states like New York and California would elect presidents. It takes a wise person about two seconds to see what a disaster that would be. If the elite money centers controlled the politics and election of the president, then the common sense, vitality, and, some would argue, sanity of the middle of the country would be taken out of the equation. Our country would fall to socialism in record time.

You would think the coastal elites would want the "little guy" to have a vote. After all, they always say they are for the little guy. But watching the 2016 election woke me up to the reality that the elite have every intention of controlling our electorate and doing all they can to eliminate the voice of the heartland.

SALTy?

A second attack on the heartland involves taxes. The coastal states were outraged when President Trump's tax reform passed, and the left realized their state and local taxes (SALT) would no longer be subsidized by taxpayers in thriftier states.

It shouldn't surprise anyone that deep-blue states like California and New York spend too much. Democrats are all about taxing and spending. Since they fleece their own citizens to fund their pet social and environmental projects, they want the support of states that have lower tax burdens—the heartland, essentially.

There was great outrage when the president changed that, because leftists love using other people's money. Rest assured, as soon as the Democrats regain power, they will restore the federal income tax SALT deduction, and the Midwest and South will again be taxed to pay for all the special projects on the coasts.

The SALT deduction burdens "red" states and relieves "blue" states. This is straight-up redistribution, only instead of the rich supplementing the poor, it is the middle class supplementing the elite rich coastal states, but they have the highest taxes and debt because of their irresponsible spending.

This is yet another way the leftist elites do what they can to punish conservatives.

They're so high!

Perhaps the most insidious assault on the heart of America is the weediest—pot.

I have noticed that it's the big states like California and New York that make the money on pot, while the heartland states, again, are stuck with the ramifications and fallout from the bad behavior, crime, and addictions of the legal states. Legal marijuana states are profiting hugely, but the heartland is stuck with the bill.

The states in which marijuana has been decriminalized tend to be the states that rely on the SALT deduction and the states where the movement to abolish or undermine the Electoral College is the strongest.

I don't know that anyone else is observing this shift, but I believe it is significant and growing.

The coastal regions want to legalize pot. But who suffers the consequences? The states that legalize the production and sale of marijuana stand to gain the revenues, but who buys the pot? Naturally, the border states bear the brunt of legalization. From increased crime, to more accidents, cost to business and industry, educational costs, medical costs, and beyond, the border states that happen to all lie in the heartland will pay the price, while collecting none of the revenues.

As the neighboring states start to incur all the costs, they will likely end up having to legalize pot just to gain revenue, to pay for the costs of what their neighbors have done.

What happens in California doesn't stay in California.

As the coastal states legalize, and their interior neighbors legalize, eventually, the very center of the country that will pay the highest price of all, and will ultimately be forced to legalize against their will.

Think about that. The pot debate is a thinly veiled way for the coast to control not only the money in the heartland, but the minds in the heartland.

THC, the active ingredient in marijuana, dulls critical thinking and produces apathy. The effect of pot on the minds of teenagers is worse. That all pales in comparison to what happens to the health of those who regularly indulge.

Cannabis has become so well known as a nutrient of some sort in popular culture and media that it seems we have conveniently forgotten the destructive nature of pot smoking.

The Cannabis and Health International Drug Policy Symposium studied the adverse effects of smoking pot on the human body, compiling research over two decades and across Europe and beyond.[3] They found that:

One in ten persons who smoke marijuana becomes dependent on it.

Driving while high on pot doubles the risk of crashing a vehicle.

Teens who smoke are 200 percent more likely to drop out of school.

Cannabis use as a teen significantly increases cognitive impairment.

Those who smoke pot have two times the risk of developing mental illness, such as schizophrenia, depression, bipolar, psychosis, etc. These numbers are even more severe when there is some family history of drug use, and if they start smoking during adolescence.

Marijuana smokers are more likely to develop chronic bronchitis.

Those who smoke marijuana as a teenager are much more likely to use other and harder illegal drugs, thus, the "gateway drug" argument holds true, even after controlling for potential confounding variables in longitudinal studies (repeated studies of the same variables over long periods).

Smoking weed has a profound effect on the likelihood that the user will develop cardiovascular disease. The exact statistics are hard to determine because most who smoke marijuana also smoke cigarettes.

Other studies suggest that smoking one marijuana cigarette is equal to smoking twenty cigarettes, and that the concentration of carbon monoxide and carcinogenic pathogens is much higher in pot smokers.[4] Cancer rates are upward of five times higher in those who smoke pot, when compared with those who smoke tobacco.

While these problems will affect those in legalized states, at least they will be collecting the steep revenues to pay for some of the damage. This isn't so for the states where pot is not legal. Thus, many will be financially forced to legalize pot, numb the minds of their citizenry, and incur loss of life because of the coastal states that originally decided to legalize the drug.

Easy math

If you are beginning to see the pattern I see, then it won't surprise you that George Soros, known for his support of the regressive left agenda, is the biggest supporter and organizer of the legalization of pot.

Why would that be?

Well, we all know that pot use causes apathy. The changes that occur in the brain while smoking inhibit the uptake of dopamine and can leave the brain unable to properly synthesize dopamine altogether. Dopamine is the neurotransmitter that regulates our pleasure center, monitoring the feelings one has when eating chocolate, having sex, laughing, or feeling motivated, to name a few examples.[5]

What could be worse than masses of people losing their motivation and the ability to feel pleasure in normal ways? Sadly, here is the answer.

Biological Psychiatry studied the link between pot and psychosis. Researchers from three London-based universities found that in particular, schizophrenia might be linked to pot use. They conducted PET

(Positron Emission Tornography) scans of the brains of nineteen users who had experienced psychotic breaks (a complete delusional break from reality) under the influence of pot.

The scans showed that those who regularly used pot have a noticeable reduction in dopamine uptake capacity in the striatum—the cluster of neurons in the middle of the forebrain, critical for motor skills, cognition, planning, decision-making, motivation, and the ability to perceive rewards—compared with non-users.

This kind of damage to the process of dopamine synthesis can cause lack of motivation (apathy) and even psychosis.

So why would George Soros be such a proponent of legalizing marijuana?[6]

We saw what Soros did when he decided he wanted to control the media—he controlled the media. Now he has declared war on the heartland. That should tell you the severity of the battle at hand.

The truth about the environmental, legal, mental, and medical tragedy of marijuana has been counter-marketed to such a degree that most Americans now think pot is a healthy choice. Soros has modeled his pro-pot ad campaign after the tobacco ad campaigns of the 1960s. It's modern. It's hip. It's healthy and sexy. It will make you feel better and relax. It could even cure you of what ails you!

Today's pot is even more potent and wreaks more havoc economically, medically, mentally, and environmentally than the pot of the 1970s.

Opioids have become big news in the media, but what is seldom mentioned is that almost all of those who are laced and subsequently addicted to opioids started their journey with the infamous gateway drug pot, many as young as the age of eleven.

It's hard to know whether apathy leads to drug dependence, or drug dependence leads to apathy. Either way, more pot smokers will mean more votes for Democrats. Whether they are voting for more decriminalization for pot users, or more social programs and free stuff for those who ultimately suffer the effects of pot, one thing is clear: pot users vote Democrat, especially those who abuse the drug. That alone is enough reason for the left to want pot legalization. More pot equals more votes, and that equals more money and power for Democrats! That's easy math.

I have never before taken a strong stand against legal pot use for adults. Maybe I lived in California too long, and I just figured if people want to do stupid things to ruin their lives, they will. Anecdotally, I have known casual, occasional pot users who lead more productive lives than many of my friends who only drink alcohol. If people can afford their own medical bills, are over the legal age, and want to grow their own pot, and use it casually or medicinally, I think of it like alcohol. Not the smartest choice, but probably not the dumbest.

Do I think pot is more dangerous than alcohol? Yes. Do I think it is as addictive as alcohol? No. Do I think pot should be legal? Not unless it is legal nationwide, so the coastal states cannot bilk the heartland. Do I think it causes apathy? Absolutely. Do I think commercial pot farming destroys the environment (including destroying the rare Spotted Owl in California)? Yep! Do I wish people would spend their time on more productive plights, like learning Western Civ or working out? I do.

But this is not a moral crusade for me. This is a societal crisis being exacted by Soros and his cronies, and that scares me to death.

Wrapping it up

If you have made it this far in this book, there is an intellectual part of your political analysis that can't go unanswered, and that curiosity brought you to this point in this book.

Continue to look for this "assault on the heartland" pattern to be repeated. The issue might change, but the general assault on the center and south of the country will not.

CHAPTER 7

FIGHTING FOR YOUR LIFE

How the Left Embraces Death

"Don't run, if you can walk. Don't walk, if you can stand. Don't stand, if you can sit. Don't sit, if you can lie down. Don't stay awake, if you can take a nap."
—Anton LaVey, Founder, First Church of Satan

"Life is winning again in America!"
—Vice President Mike Pence

Abortion

No matter where you stand on anything, it is utterly mind-boggling that we, as a nation, have stood by since the 1970s while our babies are murdered.

It is even more astonishing that we not only tolerate it, but subsidize it to the tune of $1.5 million taxpayer dollars every single day.

And to kill those babies, we subsidize an organization founded by a Nazi sympathizer, racist, and eugenicist—Margaret Sanger. In the 1920s, Sanger said that "undesirables were polluting America's racial stock." In the 1930s, she promoted a program called the "Negro Project," which was intended to reduce the size of black families.[1]

We shouldn't be surprised that today the largest killer of black people in the United States is not gun violence, homelessness, war, or malnutrition. It is abortion, by far. How is that not racist?[2]

More than ten thousand babies are slaughtered every day in American abortion clinics in the name of convenience. Most abortions are repeat abortions. When women die along with their babies, the American media sweep it under the rug. Sometimes it goes wholly unreported. How is that different from "back alley" abortions?

More "enlightened" countries in Europe are shocked by the savagery that America condones.

There are twenty women's health clinics for every one Planned Parenthood clinic in America, yet we continue to buy the lie that Planned Parenthood is needed for women's health and mammograms. (Planned Parenthood doesn't do mammograms.)

LiveAction.org reports, "The U.S. is presently 1 of only 7 nations out of 198 in the world that allow elective abortion after 20 weeks of pregnancy." The other countries that allow it are Canada, China, the Netherlands, North Korea, Singapore, and Vietnam. They point to "a growing culture of moral relativism, personal narcissism, and secular humanism that have all contributed to the moral evil of abortion."

How is it that we don't see the madness of killing babies?

A greater heinousness

In the 1990s, when my husband was in the state legislature, I learned that almost 90 percent of unborn babies who were diagnosed with Down syndrome were aborted. I became obsessed with the idea of adopting one baby with Down syndrome, which we ultimately managed to do, through the grace of God. I told that story earlier in this book. But I find it so illuminating that while the left claim to be the heroes of the "little guy," my little guy with Down syndrome, Samuel, was abortable to them.

Habit creates complacency, and it seems babies in America have met that fate. I believe that the mental damage caused by abortion in America led us down a dark path of embracing death on many levels, and I believe that embrace haunts us on every level, every day of our lives.

When *Roe v. Wade* was passed in the 1970s, we didn't have ultra-sounds. We didn't understand when babies smiled, breathed, felt pain, cried, and fought for their lives. We do now. We now know that babies born as young as 21 weeks gestation can survive. We have no excuse for what we are doing to our babies.

I believe Donald Trump understands this. It was an important factor in his political conversion. He watched as his friend fought to save the life of his unborn child, and that forever changed the way he thought of abortion. During the presidential campaign he wrote:

> Let me be clear—I am pro-life. I support that position with exceptions allowed for rape, incest or the life of the mother being at risk. I did not always hold this position, but I had a significant personal experience that brought the precious gift of life into perspective for me...
>
> America, when it is at its best, follows a set of rules that have worked since our Founding. One of those rules is that we, as Americans, revere life and have done so since our Founders made it the first, and most important, of our "unalienable" rights.
>
> Over time, our culture of life in this country has started sliding toward a culture of death. Perhaps the most significant piece of evidence to support this assertion is that since *Roe v. Wade* was decided by the Supreme Count...over 50 million Americans never had the chance to enjoy the opportunities offered by this country...They are missing, and they are missed.
>
> A culture of life is too important to let slip away for convenience or political correctness. It is by preserving our culture of life that we will Make America Great Again.[3]

Americans perceive that the slaughter of babies is not about saving lives, or helping women, or helping children. Americans sense in their bones that abortion has created a culture of death that must be reversed. The evidence is overwhelming.

Truly terrifying

Many today have been woefully lulled into complacency about terrorism because of our strong military and the great strides they have made against the persistent terror threat under the strong leadership of President Trump.

On a recent visit to Israel, I realized how amazing Israel is—this tiny country surrounded by and under constant threat from Islamist terrorists. Israel is amazing because it still *exists*!

As I laid that mental template over the West in this moment, it didn't seem very far-fetched to visualize America as the only surviving capitalist, freedom-loving, non-Islamist country if Western Europe continues to fall to Sharia law.

I am re-convicted to dissect and research terror at its roots, and in its complexity. I found some answers.

Few things are as difficult to understand as the West's refusal to acknowledge the Islamist roots of terrorism. Why do we excuse the wholesale slaughter of people simply because Sharia doesn't like them?

Take gays, frequently thrown from buildings in Islamist countries, simply because they are gay.

Take women, often stoned to death and considered one-sixth of a human being by legal standards in many Islamic countries. Women aren't allowed to vote, or drive, or be educated. In many cases, they aren't even allowed to show their faces. They are subject to arranged marriages that are often abusive. There is no escape for them. That's not even to mention the "honor killings" *in America*, that our media sweep under the rug on an almost daily basis.

To understand the psychology of those tolerating the killing, we should understand the psychology of those doing the killing.

Inside in the mind of terror—know your enemy

There is a dark psychology that lends itself to terror. The West is an inviting target for terrorists because of our acceptance of globalism and collectivism. Terrorists recruit in prisons and ghettos, where men are psychologically primed for terrorist acts.

The ancient Chinese general, strategist, and philosopher Sun Tzu wrote, "If you know the enemy and know yourself, you need not fear the result of a hundred battles. If you know yourself but not the enemy, for every victory gained you will also suffer a defeat. If you know neither the enemy nor yourself, you will succumb in every battle."

It's time we heeded this wisdom.

The greatest present threat: Islamism

Americans are aware that we are being invaded by an anti–Western Culture political group: Islamists. Though some would argue that the "radicals" are really those who reject the brutality of Sharia, while those who embrace it are actually "adherents." Whatever your stance, you can't help but wonder why so many Islamists want to be here, when our culture is so counter to all they believe.

Under President Trump, terror cells have been decimated around the world. But what is happening domestically? What is going on inside the mosques right here in America? How much influence do the dangerous Islamists who endeavor to recruit killers have in our schools, our politics, and our government?

Terrorists are able to take advantage of America's guilty conscience. We are so traumatized by the historical stain of slavery that any accusation of racial discrimination leaves us paralyzed. No one can name those at fault, even in murder. We have, as a society, become so color blind that we've made ourselves advocates of racial division and blind to reality instead.

Additionally, the atrocities committed by Nazi Germany against Jews and Christians have left us reluctant to impugn an entire "religion." The Jews, however, were never a geopolitical force before World War II, and that's a crucial distinction to keep in mind when talking about global Islamism and Sharia law. Still, Americans' healthy aversion to religious persecution makes us uncomfortable with identifying our enemies by their religion.

Human beings are born with one strong instinctual drive: to avoid death. For that reason, we avoid danger, we exercise, we cling to youth, and we try to build a legacy. This is not just a feature of Western culture. The will to live is the most basic of all human experiences, regardless of culture. Psychologists report that the most prominent characteristic of those with the greatest will to live is a sense of purpose. People who believe they have a purpose in life that is higher than self are the least likely to want to die.

So how does a political system like Islamism convince young people to commit suicidal acts of terror? It doesn't seem to make sense. Yet if you examine the psychological tactics they employ, it suddenly makes all too much sense.

Warfare of the weak

A small number of Islamist tribes cannot inflict the terror necessary to upset the entire free world, so they must recruit. But where do they find recruits? Most beneficial to their Islamist agenda is to recruit from within the areas they want to attack—generally speaking, the West. They know that radicalization can be accelerated when someone has already demonstrated a propensity for violence. The learning curve is shallow that way, and the psychology is already in place for the kill.

Therefore, prisons and gangs are their best recruiting centers. The best terrorists are those who have already shown the tendency to explode and act out violently. The Islamist recruiters know this, and are quietly working in prisons and gang areas across the world for new recruits. Many of these areas are remote. Law enforcement leaves them alone, which makes for perfect recruiting bases.

Dr. Clark McCauley says that terrorists recruit based upon an age-old theory called "warfare of the weak." The common thread seems to be alienation, insecurity, and isolation. The model of a potential terrorist is someone who will fit well in a disenfranchised group and wants to fight the political power he sees as oppressive. The difference between a mad gunman who shoots up a school and a future jihadist is that the jihadist has found a social group of societal rejects. The mad gunman hasn't.

It shouldn't surprise us, therefore, that some of the places they are recruiting now in the United States are prison cells, gang rosters, and disenfranchised minority neighborhoods.

Going a little deeper

As human beings develop, their death anxiety often evolves into a need for camaraderie, adventure, and a heightened sense of identity, according to John Horgan, Ph.D., an Irish political psychologist now teaching at Georgia State University. Using his psychological model of potential terrorists, mental health professionals are now beginning to look for the so-called "cracks" in the why, to see where they can intervene in the path to terrorism.

Horgan identifies the following characteristics in those who tend to be more open to radicalism:

They feel angry, alienated or disenfranchised.

They believe that their current political involvement does not give them the power to effect real change.

They identify with perceived victims of the social injustice they are fighting.

They feel the need to take action rather than just talking about the problem.

They believe that engaging in violence against the state is not immoral.

They have friends or family sympathetic to the cause.

They believe that joining a movement offers social and psychological rewards such as adventure, camaraderie, and a heightened sense of identity.[4]

Persons who have been recruited by Islamists with murderous intentions concur. In February 2015, Canada's Sun News interviewed

Athar Khan, a young reformed Muslim and admitted former radical. Khan got out of the radical movement by changing schools and getting out of the mosque, and was willing to talk about his experience. He says he would not have been recruited if he were not "insecure" and lacking a strong sense of identity. The mosque preyed on his inability to fit in, and the "friend" who recruited him led him gradually down the path to radicalism.

Radicalism made Khan feel like a man. It gave him a sense of purpose and belonging. He enjoyed having an identity that was contrary to everybody else around him. He started to see his strict adherence to Sharia law as making him special. Believing in his own moral superiority through Islam, he was attracted by the idea that "you're gonna be a unique, one out of a million doing the right thing…[T]hat's how they grab you with that message, and then followed by that is a much more radical message."

Khan believed that the only way to be a good follower of Islam was to believe in Sharia law, and that the only way to "excel" in following Sharia is to implement its teachings, which include violence against infidels.

The other students in his mosque were becoming more radical. One young woman "justified chopping peoples' heads off and cutting peoples' hands." She told Khan, "It's in the Qu'ran. What can I do?"

Khan knows that this will shock most Westerners, who would expect him to report such a person to the authorities. But he can't, he says, or he would be reporting everyone he talked to at the mosque he attended. "You don't go into a mosque or a Muslim student association and hear them teaching against stoning, against killing gay people, against killing apostates. They don't teach against those things. And the crowd already believes in those things. So they are completely fine with leaving them vulnerable to radicalization for an Imam to come in…and say, 'Hey guys, why don't you do what you already believe?' And that's the problem."

Obviously, not all mosques teach the atrocities that Khan experienced. But how do we Americans remain tolerant and still decipher the danger that dwells within many of our towns and cities?

What makes them tick?

Islamism, like Communism, uses collectivism to convince its followers to sacrifice more, exploiting certain characteristics identified by Jerrold M. Post, M.D., the director of the Political Psychology Program at George Washington University. The combination of a strong sense of victimization, fear of group extinction, higher moral condition than the lives of your enemy, and lack of political power to make the change you seek is the recipe for terror, says Dr. Post.

"Being part of a collectivist cause has always been a hallmark of people willing to undergo personal sacrifices," observes Arie Kruglanski, Ph.D., co-director of the National Consortium for the Study of Terrorism and Responses to Terrorism at the University of Maryland. After surveying thousands of Arabs, he and his team found that those most likely to support terrorist activities against Westerners were those with the strongest collectivist mentality. Joining terrorist groups, says Kruglanski, may confer a sense of security and meaning that people do not feel as individuals.[5]

The stranglehold of globalism

Globalism has also contributed to the terrorist mentality, according to Georgetown University's Dr. Fathali Moghaddam, who argues that a fear of cultural annihilation likely fuels terrorist sentiments. He suggests that globalization has forced on many cultures a large-scale neurotic drive to survive, forcing smaller, more disparate cultures into a chronic and intense "fight or flight" response, with an emphasis on the former choice.[6]

After I had cited Dr. Moghaddam's work in a column at WND.com, a Jordanian air force pilot was burned alive in a cage by ISIS. President Obama's response was that "climate change is a bigger threat than terror." A supposed threat like global warming may be an instrument of peace, says Dr. Moghaddam, since it theoretically threatens everyone on earth, not only one culture or country. Perhaps that's why many on the left and in academia are so fanatical about it. They're just trying to distract the terrorists!

Moghaddam says one view of Islamic terrorism is that it's a reaction to the fear that the fundamentalist Islamic way of life is under attack. But that perspective might be dangerous.

In a personal interview with me, Dr. Dathan Paterno, a clinical psychologist in Chicago, said "despite research that points to the inherent dangers of globalism and collectivism, mainstream psychologists generally promote the very traditional liberal agenda that fuels both. Instead of using their data to make a political stand against globalism and collectivism or communism spreading across the globe, they reach for other solutions that don't follow logically from credible research; unfortunately, this keeps the wool over the eyes of most Westerners."

Accepting the theory that terrorism is a response to collectivism and the resulting insecurity, Kruglanski and his colleagues have tried to suggest ways of diffusing some of the hostility of detained Islamic radicals and making them feel more secure. Their proposals have three components:

An intellectual component, often involving moderate Muslim clerics who hold dialogues with imprisoned detainees about the Quran's "true teachings" on violence and jihad.

An emotional component that defuses detainees' anger and frustration by showing authentic concern for their families, through means such as funding their children's education or offering professional training for their wives. This aspect also capitalizes on the fact that detainees are weary from their lifestyles and imprisonment.

A social component that addresses the reality that detainees often re-enter societies that may rekindle their radical beliefs. A program in Indonesia, for instance, uses former militants who are now law-abiding citizens to convince former terrorists that violence against civilians compromises the image of Islam.

Paterno told me Kruglanski's "solutions" are exactly why terror is spreading like cancer. Aside from Kruglanski's suggestion that a fear of global warming might be an answer to the radical tribalism that leads to terrorist acts, Paterno pointed to the questionable basis for Kruglanski's proposals. "The idea of paying the education costs of terrorist's children as some sort of 'peace' offering is not only upsetting, it is laughable on its face," he said. "Every bully knows he is winning when he extracts more loot from his victim. It isn't until the victim punches back—squarely and repetitively—that he gains some respect from the bully. The same is true for Islamic terrorists. Peace is non-negotiable. We need to hit back hard each time, and make them feel it. Until they hurt more critically and more consistently than we do, they will never stop."

He pushed the point further. "If we are to follow Kruglanski's idea and teach the truth of Islam's teaching on jihad and violence, we would certainly open a few eyes, because violence against 'infidels' is advised hundreds of times in the Quran. Those probably are faulty assumptions on the part of the professor, however well-intended."

Frankly, the most basic, best practices against bullies are these: never negotiate, and always hit back harder than they hit you. This is "basic bully psych 101," and that research falls in line with Paterno's arguments on how to treat terror.

Unless Kruglanski or someone else can demonstrate that the psychology of the terrorist is any different from that of the playground bully, it would be difficult to prove why doing nice things for those who want to kill you is a solution.

How terrorism flourishes

Aside from the necessary environment of globalism and collectivist political mindset, recruiters must understand what kind of personality makes a good recruit for terror. Dr. Ervin Staub, of the University of Massachusetts, cites three such personalities:[7]

Idealists. They support the terror based upon their own ability to identify with the suffering of some group that they are not even a part of. This can be misplaced.

Respondents. They support terror based upon personal experience as a member of a group being defended by a terrorist reportedly acting on the behalf of that persecuted group.

Lost Souls. They are adrift, isolated, and often ostracized. They can find a sense of purpose in a radical group, so they are "ripe for the picking."

Another psychologist, Dr. Clark McCauley, of Bryn Mawr College, names four basic trajectories of a terrorist:[8]

Revolutionaries. They are involved in a cause over time.

Wanderers. They move from extremist group to extremist group, searching for a sense of purpose.

Converts. They suddenly break with their past and become a part of an extremist movement.

Compliants. They convert to the group through persuasion by a friend, a relative, or a romantic interest.

Experts weed out the mentally unstable, meaning the truly insane (like the paranoid schizophrenic Ted Kaczynski, the "Unabomber"). Some contend that clinical insanity is not a leading indicator of susceptibility to follow a terror group, nor is it a credible defense after a terrorist crime in most cases. Moreover, terrorist leaders prefer to select those of highest status for their suicide missions, since sending those with more to lose lends credibility to their mission.[9] But given the cellular nature of terrorist groups, are we really to believe that they are administering sophisticated psychological evaluations on their terrorists before selecting their next suicide bomber?

Other professionals take exception to attributing such rational thought to Islamist terror organizers. Many argue that condoning rape, training children to kill, and oppressing, even mutilating and killing, women, is not the product of a sane culture.

Nicolai Sennels writes,

> As a psychologist in a Danish youth prison, I had a unique chance to study the mentality of Muslims. 70 percent of youth offenders in Denmark have a Muslim background. I was able to compare them with non-Muslim clients from the same age group with more or less the same social background. I came to the conclusion that Islam and Muslim culture have certain psychological mechanisms that harm people's development and increase criminal behaviour.[10]

Or is it simply that those who are immigrating to Denmark or else-where in Western Europe have come with a purpose? It goes against what I know of human beings to see others, especially whole groups of people, as "unreformable." I believe otherwise, because I know people like Dr. Zhudi Jasser, who calls upon modern-day Muslims to "declare war on radical Islam." He supports the president's ban on immigrants from countries that pose a particular terrorism threat, and he distinguishes political Islam from religious Islam.

Sennels might find Jasser's efforts somewhat in vain. He says that the typical way we deal with crime, politics, and punishment in the United States is a glaring antithesis to what is really needed to stop the war Islamic terror against the West. "Far too many people underestimate the power of psychology embedded in religion and culture. As we have already seen, no army of social workers, generous welfare states, sweet-talking politicians, politically correct journalists or democracy-promot-ing soldiers can stop these enormous forces," he writes.

Sennels says that "sensible laws on immigration and Islamisation in our own countries can limit the amount of suffering, but based on my education and professional experience as a psychologist for Muslims, I estimate that we will not be able to deflect or avoid this many-sided, aggressive movement against our culture."

The elephant in the room is the question on how to eliminate terror, and whether it ultimately involves the annihilation of Islamist terrorists. Nobody wants to talk about it, but that is the heart of the matter in this war. Those who have been hurt by terror don't want to become like their killers. Further, it is almost as if the West in general is "aller-gic" to a real conversation about the facts of the terror being inflicted on them, so that avoidance mutes the conversation that could lead to real answers.

Citizens wait on some "expert" or politician to come along and give them answers. The problem is that "experts" are human and fall short. Experts are paid and sometimes have questionable motives. And the reality is that if you can't have an honest conversation about the source the terror, then you can't then decide how to fight it. You can't defeat an enemy you won't even identify. That is foundational.

Mental health professionals around the world debate terrorism even as it grows like a cancer. President Trump has successfully reduced the Islamist terror threat in America for the moment, but make no mistake: Europe is being devoured while we are enjoying the freedom from terror our president has established here. Solutions evade professionals because of cultural, religious, and political differences that seem to meld into the perfect storm of confusion on the matter, even for the most highly trained psychologists in the world.

The trend is to point to the terrorism problem and the West's stubborn refusal to look squarely at the problem and call it what it is. The president was harshly criticized as a "xenophobe" when he used Obama's own list of the most dangerous counties to ban travel that could import terrorists. Activist courts fought him. Ultimately, travel bans, if effective, will be only a first step in the direction of true peace. Until that first step is accomplished, most are pessimistic that true solutions can be found to curb the violence that will likely affect generations to come all across the West.

Promise may lie in the fact that more and more professionals are facing the hurdle of overcoming what is deemed politically correct to face the problem from a more realistic perspective.

They say admitting you have a problem is the first step toward overcoming it. Perhaps this is a giant step for a profession that might eventually find the answer to terrorism.

The question no one will ask

"I will cast terror into the hearts of those who disbelieve. Therefore strike off their heads and strike off every fingertip of them."
—Quran 8:12

It appears that Western society may have to make some tough decisions. Historians and religious leaders in Western cultures are grappling with these decisions now.

This is difficult for a culture that has experienced discrimination against Jews, blacks, and others. Western societies have fought hard to put discrimination and prejudice behind them. So the idea of saying that the very culture of Islam leads to evil is naturally repugnant to us.

The predominant Judeo-Christian faith of America is another hurdle to painting Islam with a broad brush. Some European municipalities have said plainly that "Islam is evil" and "needs to be eradicated." This raises a question that is obviously haunting for pastors and rabbis in the United States: If you effectively "ban" Islam, what religion is next?

There are practical implications, too. A country can order Muslims to leave, but they won't all go, especially those with evil intentions. The majority of those who would leave in such a scenario would be the law-abiding, peaceful Muslims. True Islamists would hide, and imbed, and wait out the ban. So that doesn't accomplish a lot.

Additionally, vast numbers of politicians are paid off to ensure that importations of all non-Americans continues, and especially those who will disrupt our constitutional governance. The process is simple. Those who wish to break America will pay for their access, and they know how to talk to politicians who want their money. They know the right words to say and the right monetary buttons to push, and the reality is that many of the terror organizations are supported by the big oil money that is a cog in the American political system. So there is no visible end to their money stream.

More and more experts, including Muslims like Dr. Jasser, are contending that the term "religion" does not accurately describe many Muslims—that there exists a geopolitical system that seeks to overtake the West, not simply a faith. But that does little to calm the fears of true religions, such as Jews and Christians, who have been repeatedly persecuted throughout history by Islamists.

Trending thought seems to hold that to stop the killing, Islamism needs to shed the shroud of "religion" and be considered the political system that it is. Once Islamism is identified in the collective American psyche as a geopolitical system, the answers to the slaughter by terrorists seem to become clearer.

Some say that Islam is a religion, and therefore to name it as the sole proprietor of terror is to attack someone's religion. But the work of Robert Spencer, the founder and director of Jihad Watch, says that because of the politics necessary to implement Islamic Sharia law, there is no comparison to Judaism or Christianity, neither of which mandates certain forms of politics. Spencer contends that Islam is a way of life that includes a political system, despite denials of Islamic apologists.

Lt. Col. Ralph Peters gave a detailed plan to Bill O'Reilly on how he would fight terror:

> One: You accept that you are in a war. Two: You name the enemy, Islamist terrorists. Three: You get the lawyers off the battlefield.... [Y]ou accept there will be collateral damage and you do not apologize for it. You do not nation build, you don't try to hold ground. You go wherever in the world the terrorists are and you kill them, you do your best to exterminate them, and then you leave, and you leave behind smoking ruins and crying widows. If in five or 10 years, they reconstitute and you gotta go back, you go back and do the same thing, and you never, never, never send American troops into a war you don't mean to win.[11]

Col. David Hunt said that there must be economic pressure in addition to the military campaign that Peters detailed. Hunt said that just killing terrorists has not worked; "killing them is the only thing that works," Peters fired back.

Roger Cohen, a *New York Times* columnist, said this:

> I do hold Muslims responsible to this degree: I don't think that we can solve this problem...until moderate Muslims really speak out—really say, "This is not our religion. This is not something we can accept. This is absolutely barbaric.

This is the murder of innocents. This is an attack on Western democracies and the freedoms we all stand for. And we are now part of these societies. We're living in them." Until they speak out in that way, I don't think we're going to see much progress, and I think that's a responsibility they have.[12]

An anonymous Facebook user points to the record:

The Beltway Snipers were Muslims.
The Fort Hood Shooter was a Muslim.
The Charlie Hebdo killers were Muslim.
The underwear Bomber was a Muslim.
The U.S.S. *Cole* Bombers were Muslims.
The Madrid Train Bombers were Muslims.
The Bafi Nightclub Bombers were Muslims.
The London Subway Bombers were Muslims.
The Moscow Theatre Attackers were Muslims.
The Boston Marathon Bombers were Muslims.
The Pan-Am Flight 93 Bombers were Muslims.
The Air France Entebbe Hijackers were Muslims.
The Iranian Embassy Takeover was by Muslims.
The Beirut U.S. Embassy bombers were Muslims.
The Libyan U.S. Embassy Attack was by Muslims.
The Buenos Aires Suicide Bombers were Muslims.
The Israeli Olympic Team Attackers were Muslims.
The Kenyan U.S. Embassy Bombers were Muslims.
The Saudi Khobar Towers Bombers were Muslims.
The Beirut Marine Barracks bombers were Muslims.
The Besian Russian School Attackers were Muslims.
The first World Trade Center Bombers were Muslims.
The Bombay Attackers were Muslims.
The *Achille Lauro* Cruise Ship Hijackers were Muslims.
The September 11, 2001, Airline Hijackers were Muslims.

Think about it:

Buddhists living with Hindus = No Problem

Hindus living with Christians = No Problem

Hindus living with Jews = No Problem

Christians living with Shintos = No Problem

Shintos living with Confucians = No Problem

Confusians living with Bahá'ís = No Problem

Bahá'ís living with Jews = No Problem

Jews living with Atheists = No Problem

Atheists living with Buddhists = No Problem

Buddhists living with Sikhs = No Problem

Sikhs living with Hindus = No Problem

Hindus living with Bahá'ís = No Problem

Bahá'ís living with Christians = No Problem

Christians living with Jews = No Problem

Jews living with Buddhists = No Problem

Buddhists living with Shintos = No Problem

Shintos living with Atheists = No Problem

Atheists living with Confucians = No Problem

Confucians living with Hindus = No Problem

Muslims living with Buddhists = Problem

Muslims living with Christians = Problem

Muslims living with Jews = Problem

Muslims living with Sikhs = Problem

Muslims living with Bahá'ís = Problem

Muslims living with Shintos = Problem

Muslims living with Atheists = Problem

MUSLIMS LIVING WITH MUSLIMS = BIG PROBLEM

But factors other than religion and historical persecution may preclude the effective eradication of terror.

Collectivist attitudes have expanded in Western societies, especially in universities, and this may be a big part of the problem. Psychologists say that people who feel a strong sense of group identity are more likely to make risky decisions. They perceive the risk to be shared among members of their group. Thus, the stronger the group cohesion and collectivism, the bigger the risk they are willing to take. Also, collectivist members feel tremendous social pressure to conform to the desires of the collective and its leaders. The group provides their sense of identity as they further isolate themselves from the society at large. A sense of isolation and threat may be just the impetus needed to push the collectivist member to radical, risky acts, such as terrorism.

Some have speculated that George W. Bush's warning to Al Qaeda that he would "smoke them out and get them running and bring them to justice" may have been the moment that the collectivist mindset of Al Qaeda became decidedly more risky and radicalized.[13] Psychologically, naming individual terrorist sects may only make them feel more isolated, more collectivist, and more radical.

So calling terrorists simply "Islamic" or "Muslim" obscures the tribalism that may contribute to the collectivist mentality that may lead to more terrorist acts. America should begin by looking to Israel for answers. It has been engaged in this cultural battle since its inception. Even though, thanks to the attacks of our military under the solid leadership of Donald Trump, terror is on the back burner in America today, Europe and other parts of the world are being devoured. If America doesn't wake up, or the populous remains complacent or distracted, we could find ourselves in much the same predicament that struck me on my recent trip to Israel: A tiny nation surrounded by those who want to kill them.

Israel didn't choose her plight; she was thrust into it. America still has a chance to fight before that is our reality.

The solutions lie in understanding some basic historical and geopolitical realities. We must help others understand the dangers of globalism, collectivism, and communism. While those of us with a grasp of geopolitics, psychology, and history understand this, those three most dangerous elements of our time continue to grow.

Schools or shooting galleries?

I believe the same globalism and culture of death that has led us to look the other way as whole groups of people are slaughtered was launched in 1973 with *Roe v. Wade.*

If you wonder why conservatives get angry, look no further than the proliferation of mass shootings that are preventable.

According to Wikipedia, there were eight years with mass shootings in the forty-three years between the years 1929 and 1972. In the forty-four years after *Roe v. Wade*, there were thirty-nine years with a mass killing in America. What is wrong? Why can't we find answers?

I tell my children that when they are clearly failing at something, the most important thing to do is to look at their actions introspectively and try to find a better approach based on their previous failures. They are pretty good at it! They usually learn something, change something, and do better the next time.

We don't do this as a country when it comes to mass shootings. Why?

The moment we have another mass shooting, rather than act on what most Americans can agree upon, we tend to immediately polarize. We scatter to our side of the aisle on gun control. The only winners in that are the gun lobby and the anti-gun lobby. But there are always more dead Americans, and nothing is settled.

Why don't we secure our schools, churches, and concerts like we do our courtrooms and capital?

Every killing, I watch, baffled, as those most well protected by guns—politicians, Hollywood actors, and well-funded lobbyists—start talking about taking guns away from the most vulnerable in our society.

The Hollywood lot baffles me the most. They are the ones who make their lush livings creating the movies and video games that glorify violence. Do they not remember what they do for a living? Talk about crazy!

But rhetoric abounds on both sides. As I mentioned, I get annoyed as both the gun lobby and the anti-gun lobby use mass shootings to raise money to pay contentious, imbalanced bomb-throwers to insult one another on national television, further polarize the electorate, and never solve a problem. Both sides decide the other side is crazy because of the screamers on TV, and more children die.

The pro-gun crowd, understandably, wants to turn the argument about causation away from inanimate objects to the issue of mental health. "Let's just fund the daylights out of mental health, and divert attention away from guns," they seem to say.

I say that is the *most* dangerous of ideas.

To start, the mental health profession, of which I am a part, is filled with left-leaning regressives educated in ivory towers where more than 90 percent vote strictly Democrat. Do we really want them deciding who is sane, or even what constitutes sanity?

Second, if you are going to regulate guns based on sanity, ultimately that will involve some sort of review, or audit, of the mental health or fitness of those applying for guns.

We all know of the corruption of our government agencies. The NSA spies on us, the CIA colludes with political allies against candidates, the FBI didn't follow up on some forty reports that the killer in the Parkview school slaughter was going to go postal, and allegedly created an unmasking on private citizen Donald Trump, based on a fake dossier created by political enemies. The IRS targeted Tea Party groups, and other conservatives.

So let me ask you what I have asked my audiences on television many times: Which government agency would you like to audit your mental health, or the mental health of your children?

The knee-jerk reaction to refocus attention from our guns to someone else's mental health will most assuredly backfire. We have to come up with better solutions, and I think we can, if we can put aside the partisan rhetoric by the lobbyists and their spastic dividers, and turn instead to what works.

Allowing teachers to train and carry in states that allow them to doesn't mean that any teacher will ever *have* to carry a gun. Not one. What it does mean is that the next killer walking into a school won't *know* if the teacher has a gun. That is a game changer!

Allowing plain-clothes former military to train and carry in schools could be a wonderful way to keep our kids safe and keep killers guessing. It could mean that a veteran teaches your child the history of war or geography. It could bless our veterans with a great sense of productivity and purpose, while protecting our children in schools.

Single entry points and basic security should be a given.

Of all fixes tested so far, the one most easily evaluated is the idea of a "gun-free zone." Gun-free zones are welcome mats for killers.

Almost all mass killings in America occur in gun-free zones. If we must have a gun debate, then that is perhaps the most productive. But without revisiting our Second Amendment rights, I think enacting what we agree on—security, metal detectors, single point of entry, bomb-sniffing dogs in schools—might be more logical. Even more logical would be to eliminate the massive, union-based Department of Education and privatize our schools. A little competition would solve these problems in the most local ways in short order!

Sensible introspection could go a long way into preventing the crazy, but are we, as Americans, willing to climb off of our high horses and have that level of self-examination?

Does our societal narcissism preclude second-guessing ourselves? Can our massive partisan chasm be bridged? Can America look in the mirror and see what we have done to ourselves and agree to have a conversation?

In the next chapter, we will drill deeply into that. The divide is great, but it has been great before. Our narcissism is deep, but narcissism isn't fatal, and can even be productive in certain cases. Our media, however, may be the wild card in the journey to America's healing herself. The media madness may have gone too far.

CHAPTER 8

CLICKBAIT VOTERS

How the Media Inflames Division, and How We Let Them Do It

"What do we want? CLICKBAIT!
When do we want it? The answer will SHOCK you!"
—@AndyVale on Twitter

Clickbait is like the cartoon explosions we used to watch as a child—BOOM! POP! BAM!—only used to change the culture of news consumption and social media.

We have all fallen victim to clickbait. Go onto any website and see the pop-ups that say things like, "See the new fruit that is turning back the clock of aging!" or "You won't believe how Madonna looks now!" or "10 reasons you should never, ever eat this food again!" We've all clicked. We've all been that proverbial fish on the line of some advertiser who knows that, statistically, one in 874 of us will actually buy the miraculous fountain-of-youth product.

But we would like to think we are better than that. The good news is, most of us are.

Now, the left will report that conservatives are more susceptible to clickbait than liberals. But my question is always this: Who decides what is "clickbait"? Is Fox News clickbait? Is Breitbart? Newsmax? If the left gets to define clickbait, then it is no surprise that it finds conservatives falling for it more often.

My educated guess is this: since the left likes to exploit weakness for votes, it is probably better at getting those who feel weak to click their hooks. Conservatives are naturally more cynical about what news media they consume—some would even say paranoid. But if we are paranoid, then it's hard to make the argument that we are also more gullible.

When the left realized that the same tactics that get people to buy a miracle fountain-of-youth product could be used on weak-minded voters, it set out on the brave new path of clickbait electioneering.

"Donald Trump is a racist!"

"Donald Trump is coming to round you up and take you away!"

"Ex of Donald Trump: 'He raped me viciously!'"

These are the kind of headline that clickbaiters have found effective.

The reality is that most who glance over such headlines won't click to read them. Of those who do, few will believe the headlines once they see the story, but it doesn't matter. What matters is the emotional response of the weak-minded to the clickbait headlines. They may actually believe the headlines without looking to see how the facts were twisted to produce the headline.

Here are some *real* headlines:

>*"I've thought a lot about blowing up the White House."*
>—Madonna

>*"I'm a nasty woman."*
>—Ashley Judd

>*"Where is Rand Paul's neighbor [who almost killed him] when we need him?"*
>—Bette Midler

These outlandish, inflammatory statements were actually said. Yet they received very little attention from the media.

The problem for those who don't fall for the clickbait is that their protective numbness may lure them into complacency when truly horrible things are said and done.

The left preys on the gullible and easily manipulated. It preys on those who are fearful and desperate. And to stimulate that fear and desperation, it isn't above using clickbait and clickbait's sister, the politics of division. The left has even earned the nickname "Divisicrats."

The reality is that the right has no chance of keeping up with the left's clickbait tactics. Not only are the media firmly on the side of the left, but conservatives are generally skeptical of what they are told, even by their own side. It was conservatives who started the Tea Party as a rebellion against their own party. While the left circles the wagons, conservatives set up circular firing squads. And when conservatives elected an establishment-shaking president, the Republican establishment was shaken most of all.

So clickbait tactics aren't as likely to work on the skeptical conservative. But the voters on the left, some already in broken families or downtrodden in some other way, are more likely to respond to further emotional upset. The left knows this, and exploits the weakness of vulnerable to amass votes.

Identity politics—the politics of division—didn't use to be the way of the Democrat party. But the Democrat party wasn't funded by socialists back in the days of Kennedy, or even Carter.

The left would have you believe that if you simply fit into a particular demographic category, then you are *ipso facto* a victim. This is most offensive to me in the context of feminism. The reason I find the contrived division between men and women so disturbing is that I realize *I am not a victim*.

While I do believe women serve a critical role in God's design for this world, I don't believe that we're automatically worthy of praise without accomplishment, or that we're victims simply because of our sex.

Dennis Prager put it best: "You cannot be happy if your primary identity is that of a victim, even if you really are one." Yes, some women *are* victims, but making victimhood their primary identity does them no good.

Maybe that's why Hillary Clinton lost. The first woman nominated for president cried "victim" at every turn. Perhaps her own voters rejected her identity politics, and silently voted for Donald Trump. We know that married, family women voted in record numbers for Trump.

Some will say that the only women who voted for Trump were religious believers. But that isn't true. The late Christopher Hitchens, an anti-theist curmudgeon, wrote an op-ed for the Wall Street Journal in 2008 titled "The Perils of Identity Politics." He said:

> People who think with their epidermis or their genitalia or their clan are the problem to begin with. One does not banish this specter by invoking it. If I would not vote against someone on the grounds of 'race' or 'gender' alone, then by the exact same token I would not cast a vote in his or her favor for the identical reason. Yet see how this obvious question makes fairly intelligent people say the most alarmingly stupid things....

He then went one step further:

> For years, I declined to fill in the form for my Senate press credential that asked me to state my 'race,' unless I was permitted to put 'human.' The form had to be completed under penalty of perjury, so I could not in conscience put 'white,' which is not even a color let alone a 'race,' and I sternly declined to put 'Caucasian,' which is an exploded term from a discredited ethnology. Surely the essential and unarguable core of [Martin Luther] King's campaign was the insistence that pigmentation was a false measure: a false measure of mankind (yes, mankind) and an inheritance from a time of great ignorance and stupidity and cruelty, when one drop of blood could make you 'black.'

The left has successfully weaponized sensitivity and victimhood. But here's my question for them: When in history has a self-identified victim ever emerged as the winner?

The answer is *never*.

Winners win because they see themselves as victors even before their victory. Not sometimes, or usually. Always. Winners win. Losers lose. Victims are victimized over and over and over. Perhaps that is why it is so hard for downtrodden groups to break through and rise up. It isn't until they see themselves as victors that they can *be* victors.

So why is it so important for the left to divide people up by race, sex, income, even religion? Why do they need us all parsed into pieces? Might it be easier to convince small groups of people that they are victims in need of a savior? In need of a party to bring about "social change"? If you can convince a group of people that they are victims and you are their savior, there's nothing they won't do for you. Is that the definition of pure power?

I once thought about becoming a feminist. I tried to be proud of my sex. But simply being a woman is something that half the human race has...um...accomplished? If I win a coin toss, you can congratulate me for my luck, but not my skill. I didn't feel "special" simply because I was a member of the female sex.

That doesn't mean there's nothing special about being a woman. Indeed, the Bible makes it clear that God himself has placed every woman on a pedestal simply because she's a woman:

God is within her, she will not fall. (Psalm 46:5 NIV)

You will be a crown of splendor in the LORD's hand, a royal diadem in the hand of your God. (Isaiah 62:3 NIV)

She is more precious than rubies. (Proverbs 31:10 NIV)

Husbands, love your wives, just as Christ loved the church and gave himself up for her to make her holy, cleansing her by the washing of water through the word, and to present her to himself as a radiant church, without stain or wrinkle or any other blemish, but holy and blameless. Even so husbands should love their wives as their own bodies. In this same way, husbands ought to love their wives as their own bodies. He who loves his wife loves himself. After all, no one ever hated their own body, but they feed and care for their body, just as Christ does the church— for we are members of his body. "For this reason a man will leave his father and mother and be united to his wife, and the two will become one flesh." This is a profound mystery—but I am talking about Christ and the church. However, each one of you also must love his wife as he loves himself, and the wife must respect her husband. (Ephesians 5:25–33 NIV)

So being a woman is special, but only through the acknowledgement of Grace and Divine Creation.

The One Real Unforgivable: Using Children

"The state must declare the child to be the most precious treasure of the people. As long as the government is perceived as working for the benefit of the children, the people will happily endure almost any curtailment of liberty and almost any deprivation."
—Adolf Hitler, *Mein Kampf* [1]

One of the most effective clickbait tactics is to use children.

Children are used in the immigration debate to advocate for open borders. Leftists claim that if we do not allow every family with children to freely walk across the border unimpeded, then conservatives must hate children. It's truly a despicable tactic intended to allow illegal voters to invade the country to help save the dying Democrat party that can no longer win elections on the up and up.

They use the argument that we need to ban guns from homes, because they kill children. In reality, more children die in buckets and cars each year by far, but you will never see a move to ban buckets or cars. That is because the elite in Washington want to fool our society into giving up its freedoms, but they know they have to have a worthy cause, just as Hitler said.

I believe there are admirable, well-intentioned people advocating gun control. The problem is that we cannot give up more freedoms every time there is a tragedy, based on emotion. Our laws need to reflect the most deliberative and sober reason. Patrick Henry puts it well: "Where and when did freedom exist when the power of the sword and purse were given up from the people?"

That is why, in my mind, the Second Amendment is the most important of all in our Bill of Rights, as it protects all of our other rights. It "shall not be infringed." Without it, we have tyranny.

But others do agree with the elitist left on gun control policy:

"The most foolish mistake we could possibly make would be to allow the subject races to possess arms. History shows that all conquerors who have allowed their subject races to carry arms have prepared their own downfall by so doing. Indeed, I would go so far as to say that the supply of arms to the underdogs is a sine qua non for the overthrow of any sovereignty. So let's not have any native militia or native police. German troops alone will bear the sole responsibility for the maintenance of law and order throughout the occupied Russian territories, and a system of military strong-points must be evolved to cover the entire occupied country."
—Adolf Hitler

Guns are pro-woman

I am a Second Amendment advocate because I am pro-woman. My experience tells me that anyone who does not see it that way is either ignorant of the facts or anti-woman. But that wouldn't be a very nice thing to say about my gracious counterparts, so I won't. I will only say that most violent crime is committed against women, and most prevented crime against women is attributable to guns.

Same with children.

Recently, we watched helplessly as a shooter, once again, went into a school and killed seventeen people. This time it was near my new home in South Florida, just a short drive away at Stoneman Douglas High School. Children died. A teacher died trying to save them. The clickbaiters were out in full force, and we all stood by as politicians, media and lobbyists used the tragedy to digress into a gun debate.

Facts would prove that more gun laws wouldn't have changed anything. The FBI and local law enforcement were warned countless times that the killer was going to commit his crime. He was crazy. He had guns. He was demonic. He tortured animals (a telltale sign), and he was in crisis, because his parents had both died untimely deaths. He was the quintessential ticking time bomb, and adults and the government agencies they pay to protect us from evil did nothing.

Those who seem to want to dismantle our country seized the moment to astroturf a youth movement reminiscent of other dark moments in history. They talked of tolerance, but no dissent was allowed at their rally. Hollywood turned out to scream at a wide-eyed audience telling them to ban the guns that they make billions glorifying in their videos, rap music, and movies. The media spoke of harmony and peace, while they sowed enmity between parent and child, and even between grieving family members and friends.

To the casual observer, it looked insane.

The next month, an Islamic convert went to a sleep-over at his friend's house, close to the site of the school-shooting. That night, he murdered the family hosting him for the sleepover and their child, along with another boy sleeping there that night. Again, there were numerous reports to the FBI and local law enforcement that this guy was crazy, had guns, was threatening violence, and had converted to Islam. We heard almost nothing about this in the news because the murder happened with a kitchen knife, and not a gun. It's going to be tough to ban cutlery.

We also heard nothing about it because the killer was a member of an identity group—he was an Islamist. There is a politically correct current in this country that is devastating us, and complicit in murder. Therefore the media, the FBI, local law enforcement, teachers unions, and all the rest stand and applaud George Soros's exploitation of children in the #MarchforOurLives rallies and media campaign, and more people will die because they won't speak the truth, and demand real cures. It's maddening.

The same week, a school-shooting was stopped when an armed security guard confronted the shooter. He only managed to take one victim. There wasn't enough carnage for their clickbait to work. Saving lives with guns isn't a sexy headline for the clickbaiters. The story was buried that day, because if you use only liberal logic, you would have to say the gun saved countless lives that day.

But the truth is that guns don't save or take lives. People do, and people with guns can. The real weapon of mass destruction is the intolerant, politically correct, regressive, repressive socialist who would use young minds to carry out their political agenda of disarming a country to dismantle it.

The NSC estimates that in 1995, firearm accidents accounted for 1.5% of fatal accidents. Larger percentages of fatal accidents were accounted for by motor vehicle accidents (47%), falls (13.5%), poisonings (11.4%), drowning (4.8%), fires (4.4%), and choking on an ingested object (3.0%).[2]

"Examining all the multiple-victim public shootings in the United States from 1977 to 1999 shows that on average, states that adopt right-to-carry laws experience a 60% drop in the rates at which the attacks occur, and a 78% drop in the rates at which people are killed or injured from such attacks."
—John Lott

According to the FBI Uniform Crime Reports, 1992, violent crime rates are highest in the states with the strictest laws limiting or prohibiting carrying of concealed firearms for the purpose of self-defense. Specifically, the homicide rate is 49 percent higher, and the total violent crime rate is 26 percent higher in those states. The assault rate is 15 percent higher, and the robbery rate is a whopping 58 percent higher.[3]

In states with less restrictive Concealed Carry laws (more people carry firearms for self-protection), their homicide rates trend in favor of the states who allow their citizens to carry, according to FBI data (1992).[4]

In 1987 Florida adopted CCW, and its homicide rate fell 21 percent. Less than .008 percent were ever revoked over the course of six years. That is out of 204,108 permits. So statistically, those who carry guns to protect themselves and others are some of the most law-abiding citizens in the state! The narrative that "guns kill" doesn't work when you consider that Americans own half of the world's guns, and we are only 5 percent of the world's population. Yet you will almost never hear of a legal gun owner committing a crime with it.

As John Lott said so well…more guns, less crime. It's not only true, it is statistically proved, and it's a great headline to get clicks! The lefty media should try it once and see how it works!

Freedom Needs Guns

Consider this: Americans use firearms for self-defense more than 2.1 million times per year. These are the stories you never hear, because no one was hurt, or just the criminal was injured or killed. These are the lives that are saved each year. They are only numbers, until they are you, or your loved one.

The media could report on these incredibly heroic stories of self-defense each day, but it doesn't fit their narrative. Imagine the kind of clickbait headlines they could write:

Man Saves Family From Knife Wielding Thug

Grandmother Guns Down Fugitive

Store Clerk Saves Customers From Armed Robber

I would click on those headlines, but the media elite aren't interested in spreading news that doesn't fit their narrative.

Hating

Curiously enough, it is the party that weaponizes identity that voted to remove God from its platform. That's when the division began that we see today in the upper echelon of the Democratic Party.

In an email posted on the Vets for Trump website, one vet wrote:

> The Democratic Party is the world's most successful hate group. It attracts poor people who hate rich people, black people who hate white people, gay people who hate straight people, feminists who hate men, environmentalists who hate the internal combustion engine, and a lot of bratty college kids who hate their parents. However, the real secret to the party's success is that it attracts the support of journalists who hate Republicans, and therefore work tirelessly to convince the rest of us that we should vote for Democrats.[4]

In 2004, God was mentioned in the Democrat platform more than seven times. By 2008, they had reduced that number to one. In 2012, the Democrats voted to remove the words "God" and "Lord" from their party platform entirely.

It's not remarkable that the left is the godless party. Socialism has always espoused atheism. Government can't acknowledge a Savior when it wants to *be* the savior. Even Satan knows that there can be only one God. But they were so blatant about it. And once they had scrubbed God from the platform, their actions took on a godless life of their own.

Four sources told the *New York Times* that Burns Strider, Hillary Clinton's "faith adviser," was kept on staff, at Clinton's request, despite "repeatedly sexually harassing a young subordinate." Hillary's campaign manager recommended that Clinton fire Strider. Instead, he underwent counseling and the woman was moved to a new job.[5]

Many would ask what kind of candidate would keep a "faith adviser" in that capacity after claiming to champion women's rights. Many would ask why someone who runs on the platform of a party that rejects God would have a "faith adviser" to begin with.

Can the corrupt media keep this up?

What happens when the public no longer trusts the media? Well, according to polling, less than 50 percent of the people *do* trust the media. Their ratings are lower than those of Congress, and far beneath the president's approval ratings.

The old newspapers are losing subscribers every day, and the most far-left among them are laying off masses of people. Their papers don't sell anymore because no one believes them. Even the left realizes that they don't need to read the papers to believe their propaganda. The rise of social media has largely compensated for the echo chambers of the left and right. And neither is listening to the other.

This is the reason I never give a speech without a call to use social media.

There are many reasons why a conservative would not want to be on social media: time (we are doing better things!), logic (our friends don't live in our computer!), discrimination (they don't exactly love us out there—they block us, take our pages down, and shadow-ban us), and of course, privacy. Social media can know when we watch reality TV, and if they tell Aunt Margaret, she will lose all respect for us! And we don't want all our information handed out to some sales guy in a cheap suit to profit off our tastes!

Let's talk about this.

Time: Take ten minutes per day. Set a timer on your smartphone, sit down, and simply repost and share others' posts that you agree with. Social media is how Obama won, how President Trump won, and how the next president will win. Sending petitions and postcards and knocking on doors isn't nearly as efficient as being out there on social media ten minutes per day. Surely we can all afford that little investment in our time.

Which social media? All of them, but focus especially on where the up-and-coming population is. Right now, Twitter and Instagram are hot, as is Snapchat. That will all change, but for now, Facebook and LinkedIn are the over-fifty crowd. You can use them for your own purposes, but if I had to name three right now (and until there is an uncorrupted social media platform out there), Twitter, Instagram, and Snapchat are the three if you want to reach the under-fifty voter. LinkedIn is your friend if you want to reach industry professionals and corporate types. And Facebook, as confused as it is, is still the only show in town for the over-fifty lot.

Logic: Thank God you have a life, too! Most forms of social media are more addictive than heroin. Studies say that those who spend more time on social media are less happy, more stressed, and lonelier—not exactly an endorsement of all of those little armies of friends that some think live in their laptops. I remember after about eight days on Twitter tweeting, "Is there a 12-step program for this? I might need 13!" But your timer will protect you from over-indulgence and let you still have your life with your *real* friends.

Discrimination: Yes, they pretty much hate you. But you're in good company. Until we have a solid, nondiscriminatory outlet (Gab is trying, let's see if it gets there), we need to be out there, so the left doesn't become the North Korea of social media. If they never hear opposing thoughts or see that conservatives online actually don't have horns and fangs, then they may just be lost with their little dictators. We are there to help those who can't help themselves. Save the lemmings! Get on social media!

Privacy: Okay. I hear you on this. You are a conservative and you don't want people in your business. But if you have a cell phone or a computer, *they are already in your business*. They know everything, and battling out there on social media isn't going to make it any worse. You can always use a fictitious name and age, with fake city and hobbies and all the rest. You can be Minnie Mouse, for all I care. It's no one's business who you really are, and you never need to say. I bet Minnie was conservative anyway! And who knows? You might be able to convert some on the left who love Disney a little too much. Be whoever you want to be, and just think of it as a costume party for a cause.

The important thing is hitting back. I will talk more about how you can do that at the end of the book. They are the bully on the playground, daring us to punch back. When we do, they won't know what hit them. They fight with everything they have, but they "self-drain."

If they rely on identity politics and clickbait for the next election, they will lose. Again. And we will win. But we can't let up for a moment.

Polaroid: Polarized and Paranoid

"Today, 92% of Republicans are to the right of the median Democrat, and 94% of Democrats are to the left of the median Republican
—Pew Research Center, June 2014"[6]

Whatever the reason and whomever we want to blame—from the social engineers, to the identity politics peddlers, to the victim vipers, to the clickbaiters, to social media—we are completely polarized and paranoid about each other.

Once, when I acknowledged that my affinity for animal rescue probably didn't match my conservative profile, a good friend of mine commented that it's important to have views that don't fit well on "our side" of politics. "If you don't," he said, "you will fly around in little circles with one huge right (or left) wing!"

Pew Research reports that we have more friends who agree with us politically, and fewer who don't, than ever before. They say we are less likely to like people with opposing views, and that we increasingly want to live in areas with people who agree with us politically. How will we ever come together? More importantly, where does this end? Will the polarization and paranoia end in another civil war? Believe it or not, polling says that some on the left, arguably socialists who advocate anarchy, want exactly that.

I would submit that social media, social welfare, political correctness, and traditional media have set the stage for this division.

The rise of social media has allowed us to scream at one another anonymously. In the past, you might have disagreed with Uncle Ralph about tariffs or abortion, and you would have had the conversation, but you would have done so face to face. And even if you got so frustrated with Uncle Ralph's ranting that you walked out, you would have had to come back. Because family was family then, and that's just what you did.

Sometimes you and Uncle Ralph would even have a true "lightbulb" moment when you found common ground.

Today, if you're like many out there, you block Uncle Ralph and report him just for grins, and you don't invite him to Christmas dinner this year because you'll spend half your day on social media anyway.

Families rely on social welfare instead of socializing. While we used to go to family or neighbors or churches for help, we have less need for them now, because we use social welfare programs instead. Even if I otherwise agreed with the welfare state or socialist redistribution, I would detest it for what it has done to community in America.

I have a son with Down syndrome. Personally, I dislike the term "Down syndrome" (named after the physician who first identified it as a distinct condition) more than the word "retarded," which was used for years. "Down" sounds sad and depressing, and "syndrome" is a disease or impairment. "Retarded" simply means slow. I always thought of him as my pediatrician once described: "a rose unfolding slowly." No one would be offended if someone called a rose retarded, knowing it means slow. I will pick slow over depressing and impaired any day. But the political correctness police have banned "retarded," and "Down syndrome" gets to stand. Even I go along to get along on this one.

Don't even get me started on how political correctness now rules our conversations about race, women, abortion, and even culture. We are censored and we don't even know it.

We *say* we love the First Amendment, but we have abandoned it in many ways. We allow the left to tell us what is "acceptable" to say, and it makes conservatives feel censored, and angry about it sometimes.

The rules for conservatives are definitely more stringent than the rules for leftists. Any conservative can tell you that. We can't even label bathrooms "his" and "hers" anymore. Now colleges are trying to remove pronouns that refer to sex, such as "he" and "she."

It gets worse. But I can't go into it, because as a conservative, I will be maligned for merely mentioning what I know. So for that reason, and for the sake of time, I will move on. But note how the division around the whole "PC" movement has stirred up resentment between political sides.

Then there are the media, who are perhaps the most to blame.

Media gave up on objectivity sometime after Reagan, according to those who know. The investigative journalist once had a lot of street cred among conservatives until he became a captive to left-wing media group think.

Conservative resentment, however, provided a market for conservative answers to liberal bias. Conservative newspapers cropped up and Rush Limbaugh hit the airwaves, but things really changed when the little known news executive Roger Ailes established a brand new network. Fox News burst onto the scene in October 1996, and America was changed forever.

Now conservatives could migrate to a conservative network and at least hear their side of the conversation. This had to be like fresh water in a long desert walk!

Other forms of conservative media followed. Newspapers, magazines, and even homespun newsletters grabbed their piece of the pie. The internet made for even more options: online newsletters, email, blogs, and then social media.

Today, we don't have to read, hear, or watch news we don't want to read, hear, or watch. We don't have to mingle with family members, friends, church members, or neighbors with whom we disagree. Everything is labeled, and everyone is divided by identity politics and partisan particulars.

Marketing has become the unwitting accomplice of labeling, and it's as if we all exist in a matrix and really don't see where we have landed in history.

Can we change it? I do hope that we can find a peace, or at least a civil discourse.

My dad's views on just about everything are the opposite of mine. They have been all my life, and I grew up debating him, cancelling his vote when I was old enough, and choosing to dedicate my life to causes he finds errant and embarrassing.

But we still talk, and we still love each other. I credit him with my ability to carry on a diplomatic exchange with almost anyone, and I have actually won over some haters. It's not about convincing others I am right. It's about convincing others that I value their opinion. We can almost always find common ground if we look hard enough.

Isn't it better to find something—just one thing—that we can agree on, and then work on it together?

"Two lips can tell"

No one is more frustrated by how the left portrays us in the media than I am. No one resents its relentless attacks on the president I worked so hard to elect more than I do. But I also know that I have been wrong before. My opponent may be at the same stage of the journey that I was at not so long ago. And no matter how convinced I am, I might be wrong.

In Chapter One I stressed how important it is always to remember that you could be wrong. Even if you're right, you've got to believe in grace and in something my great-grandmother told me one day when I was five as we sat on her porch swing on West Ely Road in Hannibal, Missouri.

She had no way of knowing that she'd be with us for only one more year. She had no way of knowing that my first-born daughter would be her namesake. And she had no way of knowing that that magical day from my childhood would be engraved on my memory forever.

"Gina, you see that big, fat bumble bee on that sweet tulip over there?"

"Yes, Grandma Lyda, I do," I said as I felt the cold, gray floor under my toes on the big, wooden front porch of her bungalow, where I felt safest of all.

"Well, you know, Gina, that the bee can sting, right?"

"Yes I do, Grandma Lyda," I said, looking up at her delicate blue eyes surrounded by the fine "lacing" with which life adorns the faces of the wise.

"Don't you wonder why," she asked, "when we know that the bee pollinates the flowers, and stings those who threaten it, we don't just all act sweet, like the tulips? Maybe we wouldn't get stung."

I had to think. I had never wondered about that, but I went along with her, curious as to where she was going with this. She slowed our swing a bit and put her arm around my shoulders. I noticed the hand-crocheted lace on her dress and smelled her sweet perfume. "Gina, you know that big needlepoint I made that hangs over the fireplace in the front room?"

"No, Grandma Lyda, I can't remember," I admitted.

"Well," she assured me, "that's okay. Someday you will never forget it. Some day that needlepoint will hang on your wall in your front room, and then you will know what it means. Right now, only concern yourself with the tulips, and the bees that fly to them because they are sweet, like my honey pie! And do try not to get stung by the bees!"

She tickled me and we laughed as her finger got caught in the periwinkle ribbons my mama had tied in the ends of my braids that day—"to wrap me like a present for my Great-Grandma Lyda," I had thought to myself.

"Shall we go inside and see the needlepoint I made so you know which one it is when it hangs on your wall one day?"

"Sure!" I jumped off the swing and ran to open her screen door. It slammed, and then the heavy wooden door emitted a "creeeek" as I opened it and rushed inside.

We stared at the famed needlepoint together. I struggled to read it, tripping over the words, "T-t-two...l-l-i-i-ps...c-c-a-a-a-n...t-e-e-e-l...Two lips can tell!" I yelled exuberantly. "What does it mean, Grandma Lyda? Tell me! Tell me!" I jumped up and down, thinking maybe that might force the answer to this mystery about the bees and the flowers.

Then my great-grandmother put her arm back in that warm, familiar place across my shoulders and walked me over to the window. There was that big yellow bee, so busy, "kissing" the sweet honey of the yellow tulip outside her window.

"So now, my little Gina, one day this will all make sense to you, but right now, let's go into the kitchen and see if Grandma can find you some of that sweet honey pie I made for Grandpa Arthur! He won't mind if just one little piece is missing and our Gina has a big, sweet smile!"

I forgot all about that conversation, until last week.

Tragically too early, my beloved mother died. She was way too young, and I can barely accept it to this day. I will never be the same.

Not many years before that, my Grandma Necie died. I simply cherished her. She was the daughter of my Great-Grandma Lyda. For two years since my mother died, all of the earthly possessions of the three most important women in my childhood were put away in a storage unit. The only daughter and the only granddaughter on both sides of my family, I inherited everything. I couldn't even bear to look at it. The deaths were too close together, and too much burden to bear. Since I am an only child, on both sides, everything came to me. Everything was a memory to me, and everyone was gone now—everyone but me and my little family. Most of my Grandma Lyda's home was also in my storage unit, including the needlepoint that read, "Two lips can tell."

That needlepoint had hung in the "front room" first of my Grandma Necie and then of my own mother all of my life. But we never discussed what it meant, and I always wished I had asked my Grandma Lyda for the answer that beautiful spring day when the bee kept flying into the happy little tulip.

Then last week, I noticed the first signs of spring. We had moved to Southern Florida from Southern California, and I was delighted that I could tell it was spring here! In California, I was oblivious to the seasons, and there wasn't much wild life because it was desert where we lived on the beach. But South Florida is a true jungle, even close to the beach. And spring was springing!

The squirrels were busy nesting in my mango tree, baby lizards were showing up in our yard, to the delight of my little Bo, who loves them. And yes, the tulips were blooming.

As I stared out of the big picture window, coffee in hand, contemplating all of my commitments for that day, I noticed a big, fat yellow bee "kissing" the yellow tulip growing in my yard.

About that time, my little guy ran through the house with the dirtiest feet I could imagine, clutching a lizard, on his imaginary adventure in the jungle he was delighted to inhabit. He stopped and said, "Mama, why do people say you get more bees with honey?"

"Bees?" I questioned, "I've always heard *flies*…that you get more *flies* with honey."

"More bees than what?" he inquired, insisting on bees.

We were both looking at the same thing—that little bee "kissing" the yellow tulips in our new garden.

"More fl—, *bees* than those who…" My voice trailed off as I forgot what I meant to say. "Did you know that those yellow tulips are as sweet as my Grandma Lyda's honey pie? Oh my goodness, I could go for a piece of that right now, Bo!" I confessed.

He looked more confused, while offering a little smile to me.

I do try to answer all this curious boy's questions, so I turned to get my phone to do a quick search for where the saying about flies and honey originated. In my haste, my foot hit the corner of the framed needlepoint. As I looked down to check for blood or worse, I remembered my tiny toes on my Grandma Lyda's front porch all those decades ago.

My eyes slowly shifted back to the needlepoint she made. I noticed the yellow tulips in the middle of the needlepoint and the words that surrounded the tulips: "Two lips can tell."

"Two lips" was above the tulips and "can tell" below.

I remembered Grandma Lyda, and all of our family homes where this needlepoint had hung proudly. I was about to straighten a picture when I stopped dead in my tracks. "Two lips can tell."

Two lips can tell someone how loveable he is, or how wrong he is. Two lips can answer a little boy's questions or ignore them in the midst of busyness.

Two lips can kiss a lover or turn him away.

Two lips can build up or tear down.

Two lips can return love or return hate.

So why does the tulip get more sweetness with honey?

Tulips can tell.

All these decades later, Grandma Lyda and I were together once more, as we were on the porch on West Ely Road in Hannibal, Missouri, and she had finally told me about the bees and the tulips and her sweet honey pie.

Tulips can tell that they are sweeter with the bees "kissing" them than without. And if a bee approaches and you don't have the tulip's sweetness, you just might get stung!

I could hear my Grandma Lyda's voice, and so much was now clear about our special day so long ago.

Two lips can tell that we get more bees with honey than without. So speak sweetly, even when others don't speak sweetly to you. Be kind, even when you have to dig deep. Be loving, even when you want to hate. Be gracious, even when you want to condemn. And what can you say when someone attacks you, again, without merit?

Two lips *can* tell.

The next time someone starts with the "racist homophobic sexist bigot" name-calling—on social media, over the fence post, or at Christmas dinner—think of Grandma Lyda's sweet honey pie, and try it.

I am not always sweet or kind or loving or gracious. And I believe in punching the bully back when he punches you on the playground. But oh, what I wouldn't do for a piece of Grandma Lyda's sweet honey pie! Maybe there is a lesson there for all of us. Maybe we should try a little more sweetness and see if we get more bees. Or is it flies?

CHAPTER 9

THEY MAY WANT US CRAZY

Follow the Money

"The way to sell drugs is to sell psychiatric illness."
   —Carl Elliot, bioethicist at the University of Minnesota[1]

*"If all the drugs were thrown in the ocean, everyone
would be better off...except the fish."*
   —Oliver Wendell Holmes Jr., Supreme Court Justice[2]

When you are labeled "crazy," anything you say can be dismissed as the ranting of a lunatic.

In his dystopian novel *1984*, George Orwell noted that two very effective ways of controlling people are dumbing them down or convincing them they are crazy—in either case, they need "help," which is an invitation to have others run their lives.

Remember that when you consider the new movement to legalize pot. Across our nation, states are legalizing pot. This is not because of new discoveries about its not being harmful. It's quite the contrary—we know it is harmful, but many of our leaders have cynically decided they're fine with a portion of our population living their lives stoned.

It reminds one of the "soma" of Aldous Huxley's *Brave New World*, a soothing drug which had "all the advantages of Christianity and alcohol; none of their defects."[3] It might have shortened your life, but it kept you passive and happy, with no sense of guilt or hangover. An increasing number of states think that's a good recipe for their people.

And then there are prescription drugs...

Doctors would love to put me on medication to "fix" my ADHD. The so-called experts say ADD and ADHD—attention deficit disorder and attention deficit–hyperactivity disorder—affect millions of Americans, and they have plenty of drugs to treat the horrible affliction. But if you have been diagnosed with ADD or ADHD, then you already know what I am about to tell you: You have a superpower, if you choose to use it! You can do things that the rest of the world can only dream about. Your thoughts may skip around and move faster than others', but you aren't crazy. In fact, most of those labeled ADD/ADHD would not choose to give up their hyperfocus or other abilities, even if it meant more consistent thought patterns.

The obvious question is why did they label us with a "disorder"? But no one is asking that. And those of us blessed with ADHD, but lacking in self-confidence, might wonder if we're missing something, if we just can't "see" how disordered we really are.

Why would the entire mental health profession ignore the fact that ADD/ADHD is *not* a disorder but a personality trait that can be creative and healthy?

One reason is because mental health professionals are in the business of therapy. Everyone who has taken Econ 101 knows that businesses don't stay open unless they have customers—ideally, *repeat* customers. Diagnosing people with ADD/ADHD increases their number of patients. If ADD/ADHD ceased being a disorder, they would have a lot fewer patients.

The mental health profession is as driven by money as any other. Mental health professionals are no more altruistic than truck drivers, lawyers, or stockbrokers. Every one of us offers a service. Every one of us does it to make money. That is hard to do without a repeat customer. And some of us are corrupt.

Some get big money. Some want more money. Some are totally insatiable for money, and focus on getting billionaire investors, *like the government*, to fund their businesses. If you do it as well as Planned Parenthood (1.5 million taxpayer dollars per day), then you have yourself a cash cow! The drug companies have figured that out.

But I have figured out that thanks to my "ADHD," I can stay up for days if I decide to, with no drugs and be massively productive. I can drive through the night and write half a book or a dissertation in a week or two. The trade-off is sleeping less than is good for me, sometimes feeling a little agitated, and often not thinking in a linear way (in other words, being creative—as if that's a curse!). Instead of diagnosing so much of our society with some kind of "attention disorder," maybe we should be looking for the *advantages* ADD and ADHD can bring to people rather than drugging them.

The realities

Take Greg. Greg was eight when he was diagnosed with ADHD. His teachers didn't like his constant need for activity and called him "distracted." They said they couldn't handle him at school and that he likely needed help.

Doctors prescribed a medication that would help control his hyper behavior. His mother was hopeful, and his teachers were relieved. Greg knew he wasn't good at math—or at least he wasn't interested in math—so he was unable to motivate himself to study it, and he became distracted and anxious when he had to work through a long formula.

Greg's mom was concerned about the effects of drugs on his young brain, so when the school refused to continue to educate him without medication, she brought him home to educate him. He never got good at math, but one day, watching election returns with his dad, he found he had uncanny ability to identify voter trends; he might never excel at algebra, but he did excel at analyzing polling data. Greg eventually became one of the top political consultants in the country. He hired statisticians to do the math for his business, polling experts to break down the races, and accountants to handle his taxes. He hired a personal assistant to pay his bills and a payroll firm to handle accounts payable.

He analyzed like nobody's business, and built a multi-million dollar political consulting firm.

Greg's ADHD certainly provided challenges, but it also provided him a livelihood because he learned how to turn his ADHD capabilities into superpowers.

People joked that no one knew how Greg made it through life with his lack of concentration, but no one could deny his success, even though they couldn't understand how it happened.

Greg knew he had a superpower.

He was thrilled with his superpower. Even when he became frustrated—with all the things he couldn't do and his difficulty concentrating—and considered seeking medical help, he always chose to live with his frustrations rather than taking drugs that would deaden his superpowers.

Or take Maria. Maria was eight when she was diagnosed with ADHD. Her teachers didn't like her constant need for activity and called her "distracted." They said they couldn't handle her at school and that she likely needed help.

Doctors prescribed a medication that would help control her hyperactivity. Her mother was hopeful, and her teachers were relieved. But although her "symptoms" went away, Maria's personality deadened. Unfulfilled and unhappy, she eventually turned to alcohol and drugs to maintain that familiar, safe, deadened feeling, and ultimately, Maria drank her life away. I believe that if she hadn't been medicated, if she had learned to put her ADHD to good use, as Greg did, she too could have enjoyed success and happiness.

I speak from experience. I *like* ADHD drugs. They make me temporarily euphoric—and they keep me thin! But I know that if I take them, I lose many of the things that distinguish me as a person. And the next day, if I don't take more, I feel very dark. I believe ADHD drugs are all too similar to drugs that are currently illegal. We know they are addictive and harmful.

For many "disorders" like ADD and ADHD, drugs are not the answer; they are part of the problem.

Diagnosing for dollars—is half of America crazy?

Labels matter. The American Psychiatric Association's *Diagnostic and Statistical Manual of Mental Disorders* (DSM) is broadly accepted as the gold standard in psychiatric diagnosis. The fifth and latest edition of the manual, *DSM-V*, includes a plethora of new diagnoses for mental disorders. Temper tantrums, for example, are now diagnosed as "disruptive mood dysregulation disorder." Natural grief following a tragedy or loss is now diagnosed as "major depressive disorder." Some "disorders," like Apathy Syndrome, Internet Addiction Disorder, and Parental Alienation Syndrome, are not based on any sort of research or professional literature and seem to be the product of the lively imaginations of the editors of the *DSM-V*. Overeating is now "binge eating disorder," and forgetfulness is "mild neurocognitive disorder."

According to the *New York Times*, there is even a new diagnosis called "Sluggish Cognitive Tempo," which could be applied to some two million children whose "disorder" is that they act like daydream-y children! As silly as that sounds, big pharma jumped right on board. Eli Lilly is investigating how some of their existing drugs might "treat" this new disorder.[4]

The DSM carries a lot of weight with clinicians—who use it to diagnose and label disorders—as well as with researchers, psychiatric drug regulation agencies, health insurance companies, pharmaceutical companies, courts, and lawmakers.

Now that the definitions have been so radically expanded, *DSM-V* could label nearly half of all Americans with a diagnosable mental illness. That is up from less than 6 percent under the *DSM-IV*.[5]

Diagnosing for power

There are political as well as financial reasons for labeling people with alleged disorders. Every label creates an interest group that can become a recipient of federal funds. But also, being diagnosed with mental illness can be used as a reason to deny people rights.

For instance, in some states former members of our military diagnosed with post-traumatic stress disorder (PTSD) stand to lose their Second Amendment rights—and yet some ninety percent of combat veterans are alleged to report some symptoms of PTSD. It is certainly wrong that combat veterans who have defended us abroad should have their right to defend themselves put at risk at home.

But there are already efforts underway to prevent anyone with a diagnosed mental disorder—that could include ADD/ADHD or PTSD—for purchasing a weapon for personal protection. Yet even Jonathan Metzl, an MSNBC psychiatrist who supports increased background checks and broadened gun control measures, admits that "psychiatric diagnosis is not a predictive tool...[and] the types of information garnered in background checks is far-and-away more relevant for predicting gun crime than is a person's psychiatric history."[6]

If the state can take away your Second Amendment rights based on your mental health diagnosis, it won't be difficult for them to take away other rights, as well. This is one reason why it is so dangerous to believe that half of Americans could have a mental disorder.

Some groups have woken up to the threat, including the Citizens Commission on Human Rights International, a mental health industry watchdog, which has been one of the leaders in the fight against over-diagnosing and over-medicating alleged mental illnesses.

The CCHR is certainly controversial. It was founded by the Church of Scientology (to whose doctrines I do not subscribe) and the psychiatrist, libertarian, and non-Scientologist Thomas Szasz. Over the years, the CCHR has done some of the best and most thorough documenting of the unholy alliance between Big Pharma and the psychiatric profession.

The Commission noted: "While even key DSM contributors admit that there is no scientific/medical validity to the disorders, the DSM nonetheless serves as a diagnostic tool, not only for individual treatment, but also for child custody disputes, discrimination cases, court testimony, education and more." Moreover, the commission contended, the DSM "is driven not by science, but instead caters to the pharmaceutical industry."

It gets worse.

The Commission notes that for each item on the "expanding list of 'mental disorders'—voted into existence, not discovered as in real medicine...a psychiatric drug can be prescribed and insurance companies billed. That big formula spells big profits for psychiatrists and drug companies. And this has been exposed more recently with a U.S. Senate Finance Committee investigation into the APA [American Psychological Association] itself and the fact that about 56 percent of its $12 million-a-year income derives from drug makers."[7]

So convinced are doctors that mental disorders are rampant that according to the U.S. National Library of Medicine at the National Institutes of Health, 72.7 percent of prescriptions for antidepressants are given *without a diagnosis*.[8] Apparently it is simply assumed that mental disorders are widespread and should be medicated. This is good news for pharmaceutical companies, but not for patients.

Carl Elliot, a bioethicist at the University of Minnesota, told the Citizens Commission that the issue isn't complicated. "The way to sell drugs is to sell psychiatric illness," he said.

Kelly Patricia O'Mear, a former congressional staff member, concurred. "Drug companies pull a mental disorder out of the DSM hat and get FDA approval to use an already existing drug to treat it. Well-known psychiatrists are enlisted to publicly affirm the disorder as a social problem... *Viola*! Confirmed psychiatric ill and magic pill."[9]

The commission noted, "Of the panel members that reviewed which disorders would be included in the fourth edition revision of DSM...more than half had *undisclosed financial links to Big Pharma*. For the so-called mood disorders ('depression' and 'bipolar') and 'schizophrenia/psychotic disorder,' 100 percent of the panel members had financial involvements with drug companies. Sales of the drugs prescribed for these (by virtue of their inclusion in the DSM) reach more than $80 billion worldwide."

The commission was blunt: "Apparently, the APA psychiatrists did not want to give up this cash cow. For the DSM-V revision, another study found that 18 of the 20 members overseeing the revision of clinical guidelines for treating just three 'mental disorders' had financial ties to drug companies, with drug treatment for these disorders generat[ing] some $25 billion a year [in the U.S. alone]."

The report continued: "As the diagnoses completely lack scientific criteria, anyone can be labeled mentally ill, and subjected to dangerous and life-threatening treatments based solely on opinion.... Therein lies the underlying problem of DSM—it isn't a medical diagnostic system. It's all based on opinion—and faulty at best."[10]

The magazine *Psychology Today* agrees that "the DSM-V could possibly give drug companies running room to continue their disease mongering...hyping questionable DSM ills as a means of pushing pills."[11]

There is also the question of civil rights. In an interview with WND, clinical psychologist Dr. Dathan Paterno said he has witnessed many patients hospitalized against their will. "The psychiatric establishment has enormous power," he said. "The power to label brings the power to hospitalize and prescribe, forcefully if deemed necessary by the psychiatrist. This power metastasizes into denial of liberties. For example, I know several veterans who can no longer own a firearm, simply because they were hospitalized. Often this was due to medication errors – ironically caused by the psychiatrist."[12]

Dr. Gary Greenberg, a psychotherapist and author, points out that "Only about 4 percent of violent crimes are committed by mentally ill people. We are not going to diagnose our way to safety." Indeed, over-diagnosis, and over-medication of drugs with serious side-effects, is itself a serious problem.[13]

The *Guardian* noted: "Changing the definitions of disorders alters who has them. That affects who gets drugs and other support, and [whose] interventions are trialed on. If the criteria for attention deficit hyperactivity disorder (ADHD) are broadened, then more people are likely to be diagnosed with the condition."[14]

In 1952, the DSM was a tiny spiral-bound handbook. By the 4th edition, it was almost 1,000 pages. Is America suffering from a widespread crisis of mental illness, or is the real problem a widespread over-diagnosis and over-medication of ever-expanding and arbitrary definitions of mental disorders not based on any solid science? I think the latter.

The problem, some say, is that all the drugs being prescribed for the ever-increasing number of disorders have side effects, and drugs that effect mental states are used to treat the disorders, thereby exacerbating the numbers of diagnosable problems.

Unlike other disease models that require evidence to prescribe drugs, mental disorders don't. In fact, some contend that the very basis for diagnosis is faulty. In my research, I never found confirmation of any data that proves psychiatric conditions are even caused by a chemical imbalance. Very little chemical evidence is ever even tested, yet when doctors assign medications, a "chemical imbalance" is almost always noted, along with an unproven drug solution. Since there aren't fully objective (research based, proven) tests for mental disorders, there is very little clarity on the matter. Worse, many times unproven drugs are prescribed with little or no therapy for the patient.

The trend is evident

According to the Centers for Disease Control and Prevention (CDC), American drug use has increased dramatically over the last decade, and Americans are spending more money than ever on prescription drugs. Between 2000 and 2008 alone, Americans doubled their spending on prescription drugs.

Those numbers raised eyebrows at the time. As the Citizens Commission on Human Rights reported, "In March 2009, the American Psychiatric Association announced that it would phase out pharmaceutical funding of continuing medical education seminars and meals at its conventions. However, the decision came *only* after years of controversial exposure of its conflict of interest with the pharmaceutical industry and the U.S. Senate Finance Committee requesting in July 2008 that the APA provide accounts for all of its pharmaceutical funding. Despite its announcement, within two months, the APA accepted more than $1.7 million in pharmaceutical company funds for its annual conference, held in San Francisco."[15]

The influence Big Pharma has wielded over the psychiatric profession is enormous—and has a direct impact on patients. In 2007, the *New York Times* reported that "drug company payments to psychiatrists" in Vermont "more than doubled...to an average of $45,692 each from $20,835 in 2005. Antipsychotic medicines are among the largest expenses for the state's Medicaid program."

The *Times* report continued: "Over all last years, drug makers spent $2.25 million on marketing payments, fees and travel expenses to Vermont doctors, hospitals and universities...The number most likely represents a small fraction of drug makers' total marketing expenditures to doctors since it does not include the costs of free drug samples or the salaries of sales representatives and their staff members. According to their income statements, drug makers generally spend twice as much to market drugs as they do to research them."

The result of all this marketing? Skyrocketing antipsychotic drug prescriptions to children, even though, as the *Times* noted, for children many of these "atypical antipsychotic" drugs are "especially risky and mostly unapproved."[16]

The *New York Times* also reported that in the period between 2006 and 2008, 75 percent of donations to the National Alliance for the Mentally Ill, amounting to $23 million, came directly from drug makers.

From 2000 to 2005, payments from Big Pharma to psychiatrists rose more than 600 percent and—not coincidentally—prescriptions for children's antipsychotics rose about 900 percent. That was more than 6 times the rate that the same drugs were prescribed to children in Britain. Are American children six times more psychotic than British children? Are American psychiatrists six times more effective in diagnosing and treating children's psychoses? Or are American Psychiatrists on the take from Big Pharma?

The evidence points to corruption.

The fault lies not with people who have ADD or ADHD or who have suffered from post-traumatic stress disorder. It lies with those who think that half of Americans are crazy and need to be medicated. Don't believe it. What most of us really need aren't drugs, but faith, family, friends, and a determination to make the most of our unique gifts.

Many opioid addicts and deaths result from innocent use at the prescription of a doctor who never warned them about what to do if they become addicted, how to wean from the drug, or that they don't have to take them if their pain isn't present. How ironic is it that the FDA, which seems to speed through approval for the latest big pharma pill, is the same agency that resists releasing experimental drugs to those in critical need of them, with nothing to lose?

President Trump is not only addressing the opioid issue, he has already signed the "Right to Try" bill into law to allow those in most critical need to try new drugs, even if they aren't FDA-approved. That is a glorious step in the right direction. But the corruption of the medical lobby, the psychological lobby, the DSM committee, Big Pharma, and the FDA all need to be investigated and addressed to right this ship.

PART THREE

THE CURE
FOR CRAZY

CHAPTER 10

CRAZY LIKE A FOX

The Making of the Most Extraordinary President in History

"Narcissus weeps to find that his Image does not return his love."

—Mason Cooley

The questions I am most frequently asked on TV are: Do you think President Trump is crazy? A narcissist? Fit for office?

My answer to all three questions might surprise you: Yes.

But first, a disclaimer: It is impossible and unethical to diagnose someone without a full, clinical diagnostic, workup, which includes various inventories, interviews, and analysis. This is known as the "Goldwater Rule." Perhaps it won't come as a surprise that Donald Trump is not the first Republican the left has tried to dismiss as a nut job. It's so much easier than making an argument.

On the eve of the 1964 presidential election, a now-forgotten magazine published a "poll" of some 1,200 psychiatrists who opined that Barry Goldwater was mentally unfit to be president. After Goldwater was awarded substantial damages in a defamation suit, the American Psychiatric Association responded with a new ethical rule against offering a professional opinion about a public figure one hasn't examined.

That's a principle I take seriously, although many inside and outside the mental health professions publicly babble on about the president's mental fitness. Indeed, twenty-seven psychiatrists, psychologists, "and other mental health professionals" have defied the Goldwater Rule with a bestselling book in which they diagnose Donald Trump *in absentia* with every disorder, from "unbridled and extreme present hedonism" to "sociopathy."[1] This is speculation, not diagnosis.

Though I have spoken with the president socially, I have never had any sort of clinical access to him, nor have I had any access to any inventories he may have taken, nor have I ever interviewed him in a clinical capacity. In fact, I don't even do clinical work. I am a researcher and I have done counseling, but I only do so far charities today. Still, my gut instincts, which have nothing to do with my professional training, are pretty solid.

If I do think the president is crazy, I think he is crazy like a fox. Crazy capable of running this country, if the left and establishment would just get out of his way. I think he is crazy smart, crazy resilient, crazy capable, and crazy passionate about this country.

Do I think he is a narcissist? He could be. But I think narcissism is almost a prerequisite for success in politics. I'm not sure you can get to the higher rungs of politics (or anywhere else) if you aren't somewhat narcisstic. It comes in handy in plenty of other fields as well. I think most media stars have some form of narcissism. I actually think narcissism can be used for good, as I will explain presently.

But there are different levels and kinds of narcissism. The field of psychology needs to catch up on the anecdotal evidence out there right now, but I believe that some forms of narcissism actually translate into phenomenal ability and motivation that can serve people or causes well—even charitably.

Narcissism, like autism, is a spectrum, in my observation—it appears in varying degrees and varying forms. I think some are good, some are bad; some are safe, some are dangerous; some are pertinent, some are irrelevant; some affect jobs and relationships, and some are negligible. The term "narcissism" is overused and under-defined.

This won't surprise my enemies, but in testing during graduate school, I was found to be somewhere on the narcissist spectrum. It never really bothered me. I believe that most *everyone* falls somewhere on the spectrum, if he is honest on the inventories. Narcissists often have an inflated sense of entitlement or self-importance. I believe there is a narcissism that is perhaps more convinced of its own ability to discern truth and justice than others. I think that self-assuredness actually aids those who choose to go into law-and-order professions and, in some cases, politics or political media too. I think I fit into that category, and I think the president might, as well.

There is a darker side of narcissism, of course. The megalomaniacal, often called "malignant" narcissists, cannot see their own faults, cannot empathize with others, and blame others for their failures and misfortunes. That is a dangerous kind of narcissism. I do not believe the president fits in that category for a multitude of reasons.

I have personal experience with a megalomaniacal, malignant narcissist, and that person is still active in public today. Very few realize that this person isn't who they believe her to be or who she says she is. She harms those she purports to help. She tears down, blames, sues with abandon, and moves on to the next vulnerable victim. There is no loyalty that isn't based on her need of that person to get to her next goal. The dangerous forms of narcissism, such as this person, are not based on confidence, they are based on a deep, disturbed insecurity that becomes obsessive in nature and is motivated by jealousy, mistrust of people, fear of failure. People like this lurk in the dark crevices of Hollywood, politics, sports, and the media, but they can work common jobs, too, and weave their dangerous webs anywhere. They almost always self destruct in the end, and often in suicide. Their own obsession to prove themselves worthy, but knowing inherently they aren't worthy because they don't actually care about anyone else, even their own children, leads to their inevitable demise. Sometimes that is prison, sometimes a mental institution, sometimes suicide or worse.

The reason there seems to be an abundance of dangerous narcissists in Hollywood, politics, sports, and the media is that those fields are particularly appealing if your sole desire is self-promotion, power, money, or fame. The true megalomaniac doesn't just desire power and money, he *feeds* on it. He craves it as an addict craves heroin. He fears the slightest failure with almost paralyzing terror. He is anxious if he is not the most important person in the room at any event. He will do anything to get what he wants, with no regard for his own family's needs, let alone those of others.

There is a massive difference between the benign narcissist who is confident in his abilities and someone who harms others with abandon for self-promotion or to amass power, money, or fame.

It's important to understand the differences. I believe that if the president is a narcissist, it is the best form of narcissism. I believe there is plenty of evidence that, in fact, the president cannot be a dangerous sort of narcissist.

Narcissistic personality disorder

The underlying insecurity of narcissistic personality disorder (NPD) is thought to originate in abuse or neglect early in life. Though theories vary, NPD—which is listed in the fifth edition of the *Diagnostic and Statistics Manual of Mental Disorders* as a mental disorder—is generally thought to include an obsessive preoccupation with personal power, to the point of being destructive.

According to Dr. Allan Schwartz of MentalHelp.net, there are differences between basic narcissism and NPD. Someone like Steve Jobs or Bill Gates may have some narcissistic traits, but he's a far cry from a true NPD case like Hitler, Stalin, or Mengele. Those persons are mentally ill and quite different from everyday, non-threatening narcissists. Dr. Schwartz thinks, as I do, that some forms of narcissism can be healthy.

Donald Trump's significant childhood

Donald John Trump was born in Queens, New York, in 1946. His parents, Fred and Mary, whose photos adorn his desk in the Oval Office, probably never dreamed that their high-energy little "Donnie" would one day occupy the White House. But I bet they knew from an early age that he would do important things. As a mother of five and a former elementary school counselor, I can assure you, you see such differences at an early age.

Fred was a builder and developer who enjoyed constructing houses and apartments for low- and middle-income clients in Queens and Brooklyn.

Donald Trump was successful even as a boy. He excelled academically, but he was also a star athlete and a competent leader at New York Military Academy. He graduated high school in 1964.

A successful man himself, Fred Trump had high expectations for his fourth child, Donald, who worked construction in the summers between high school and college while his military school friends enjoyed lavish vacations with their parents. Many years later, Donald's own children would recount that he made them work hard every day, giving them an understanding of the value of money and how to earn it. They credit the strict but supportive upbringing of Donald's parents and the family's legacy of hard work.

Donald Trump first attended Fordham University but eventually transferred to the Wharton School at the University of Pennsylvania, receiving a degree in economics in 1968. By all accounts, the future president was parented well, if strictly, and as a result became a well-adjusted, self-assured business man who would accomplish great things.

This is only one reason why I believe it would be difficult for anyone to make an argument that the president is any form of dangerous narcissist. He has no tragic childhood experience. There is no record of abuse or neglect. There is no record of animal abuse or torture or anything that normally is evident in the more dangerous forms of narcissism, as some claim. He doesn't demonstrate the antisocial behavior of most narcissists, who generally avoid people and unknown environments, such as campaign rallies with tens of thousands of people that the president seems to thrive on. A narcissist is worried that someone might "see through" and expose him, , so he is carefully scripted and private, even if he has to live a public life to feel legitimate. The president is over-transparent, if anything. He seems to have no fear of being himself, even when it causes him problems later. He rejects the teleprompter and fancy consultants. He is known for calling perfect strangers up on stage and giving them his microphone. None of these things would be common-place with a darker, more mentally imprisoned narcissist.

Almost without exception, dangerous narcissists are antisocial and rebellious in childhood, and especially by high school. Donald Trump was popular with his peers and successful in almost all he attempted. These are not the characteristics of a mentally ill person. In fact, his childhood experiences, strong parents, birth order, popularity, social finesse, and academic success would indicate a well-adjusted, socially comfortable, all-American kid with a bright future.

The typical malignant, antisocial narcissist would never jump into social activities as Donald Trump always has, and still does. Narcissists send their people to control the variables and won't linger amid the fray, because they feel above it all and entitled to separate themselves physi-cally. This president is anything but that. He seems to thrive on the energy of his supporters. He even invites his enemies to have a seat at the table—with cameras!—and is almost always in a good mood.

When President Trump is off work, he usually heads to Mar-a-Lago with his family and friends. I've watched him for hours. He laughs, jokes, and enjoys that time. He invites those he knows in the room to come over to his table, calling them across the room to come say hello. He engages transparently and authentically. He lavishes praise on others. That is not the behavior of someone deeply troubled.

We have all heard tales of true sociopaths and their erratic behav-ior. From Hitler, to O. J. Simpson, to speculation about George Soros, their troubled childhoods and depressive behavior are well documented. Truly troubled people have truly troubling behavior. They tend to become reclusive, reactive, angry, antisocial, and obsessed with control. As far as we know, President Trump has never demonstrated any of that behavior.

Every time I have seen him socially, he asks if I have everything I need, if I am enjoying myself, and if there is anything he can do for me. He is incredibly warm, welcoming, happy, and engaging. These are not the traits of a malignant narcissist, or even someone with narcissistic personality disorder.

Those who know him well say the same thing: To know him is to love him. He is likeable, warm, and eager to give to others. He's human. He isn't a saint. But he gives graciously, loves deeply, and is fiercely loyal.

I have seen the president abandon his own agenda to help others. I have seen him divert from an important political event to embrace a hurting Angel Mom, or to hear someone's story of losing a loved one to opioids. I have seen him demand that his motorcade pull over to take someone he saw along the side of the road to lunch. I have seen him stay at events later than any professional political handler would allow, just to give everyone a welcoming ear. That is simply not the behavior of someone who is dangerous. That is the behavior of someone who is confident, yes, but not entitled. That is the behavior of someone who wants to achieve, yes, but for reasons he believes are for the good of others more than himself. That is the behavior of someone who wants to make a difference—not for *himself*, in his seventies, when he could retire and live the life of a king surrounded by those who love him. I see the president sacrifice his golden years for his children, his grand-children, and the future of America. I see someone willing to sacrifice all, in an almost Christ-like manner (as we all should aspire to), for us, because he genuinely loves people more than self—and his country more than self.

If the president has a brand of narcissism, it is likely a "healthy nar-cissism," the kind that exudes confidence and believes in winning. When that same person is motivated to give to others, and to win for others, it really should have a different name—stronger than self confidence—but far more self-motivated than narcissism. Maslow's "self actualized" seems to fit well. I believe this president could never accomplish all he does for his family, or his country, if he weren't self actualized.

As a "lonely only" child, I have always been fascinated by birth order, especially since I met my husband. He is the third of three boys, with a mom and dad present, and in traditional roles. That well-adjusted, easy going peacemaker who is tremendously self-assured and loves people is exactly who he is, every day, in every realm of his life. His cup is always half full.

I remember one of my children asking if she was ever supposed to feel really "happy." Experts are divided on the answer to that question. Some say that, yes, certain people do have brain chemistry that makes them feel genuinely happy most days. Others say that is a romantic notion, or at least not realistic for many. They say that although the average person will experience moments of natural euphoria, daily happiness is not a practical goal. I shared that view until the day that I told my daughter I felt that way.

My husband disagreed with me. He said that he feels happy almost all day, in all circumstances, every day. He acknowledged melancholy feelings when he was missing his dad or when he felt sad for someone else's pain, but he said that even in his own struggles, he feels basically happy.

I was flabbergasted. I couldn't imagine a daily, almost constant feeling of true happiness. But I wasn't surprised, because he often smiles and laughs in his sleep.

What is it that makes some people see the world one way, while others see it so differently? There is a lot behind that question, but let's see if we can break it down, at least where Donald Trump is concerned.

The significance of birth order

I asked others about their happiness, their personality, and their birth order. I realized that birth order seems to play a profound role in situational happiness, at least in my own anecdotal research. In fact, birth order seems to be the foundation for all other factors that create and define the psychology of the person.

I think birth order may be the reason for the president's foundational optimism. He is a rare "double birth order," according to some experts on birth order, like Dr. Robert Hurst, the author of *Life's Fingerprint*.

To be a double birth order, a person must have at least four siblings in his family of origin, and there must be a gap of at least four years between himself and the child just ahead of him in the birth order. Additionally, according to Hurst, the fifth child has to be born within three years of the sibling in question.

Here is the layout of the Donald Trump family of origin:

Parents: Fred and Mary, married.
Children:
Maryanne, born 1937.
Freddy Jr., born 1938 (died of complications from alcoholism in 1981 at age forty-three)
****
Elizabeth, born 1942.
****
Donald, born 1946
***
Robert, born 1948

Four years (represented above by asterisks) separated the births of Freddy Jr. and Elizabeth. Another four years separated the births of Elizabeth and Donald. This is where the double birth order occurs for President Trump. He likely enjoyed the attention given to the "baby" of the family while also being the older brother to Robert. So he's both the "baby" and the "oldest."

I knew this personality well, even before I knew it applied to the president.

My son Bo would have been our fourth born, but we adopted a son with Down syndrome, Samuel. Because Bo does not have Down syndrome, he gets to be the mighty leader and protector of his brother Samuel. But he also enjoys the attention and doting of being one of the youngest in our family, with a long gap (four years) between himself and his next-oldest sibling, Jack.

From the moment he was born, Bo has been the most self-confident, assertive, happy, driven child I have ever known. He masters everything he tries, and he is fearless. He has a deep compassion for people and animals, and his protectiveness of his brother Samuel gives him a strong sense of leadership and confidence in that role. He often gets into trouble when he speaks too transparently, because he competes with adults or older siblings who are trying to speak, or because he is too loud.

This is the precise description of the double birth order fourth-born child in research. Hurst writes:

> They are usually educated by their older siblings and are very outspoken. Having much older siblings they are not intimidated by older people. They like to be taken care of... [but] why are they so loud? As the baby, they need to be heard as they are overshadowed by their three older siblings. They believe life should be fun![2]

My living example of this is Bo. He wins at everything he tries. He competes hard. He spends money on others and loves seeing their reaction, but he has already saved thousands and is well invested (through my app and with parental supervision) in the stock market. He couldn't wait to be on Twitter so he asked me to open an account for him that we manage (he has no internet access at all), but he has quite the enviable following, already!

Donald Trump was a gifted athlete and almost played professional baseball. The fourth-born loves to compete and finds joy in the competition.

Reports say that he enjoyed competing with Ivanka, a professional skier. She challenged his skiing skills, and he seemed to appreciate that about her. And Dr. Hurst points to the professions Trump has pursued: he's owned golf courses, resorts, casinos, and beauty pageants. The fourth born likes to make life fun!

So what about when he tweets, and the establishment goes mad? What about when he talks down to those we think are important? Hurst contends that this is the "baby" birth order, asserting himself among his older siblings and making sure he is heard. I see this every day in our Bo, and I just laugh when Bo has audience with the president. It's like they are on their own amazing planet and the rest of us only wish we could be what they are! Knowing Bo helps me to feel like I understand the president in ways, perhaps I wouldn't, if I didn't love a little guy who exhibits so many of the same characteristics he does.

It should be noted that the president says he has never smoked or had a drink of alcohol. Obviously, the death of his brother Fred Jr. greatly influenced his own decision to live soberly. Fred died of complications related to alcoholism as a young adult. The president never forgot that, and made a decision early on to abstain from the substance he believes killed his brother. This is both admirable and healthy. But more than that, the president seemed really to relate to the people he met on the campaign trail who told him their stories of losing loved ones to opioids. The way he integrated those heavy life experiences into action says a lot about how mentally fit this president is, and about his ability to take the tough times in life and use them to better his own life and the lives of those he can help. That's winning.

But where does his firstborn birth order category come into play? One thing is for sure, firstborns like to be in charge. They also identify with the dominant parent, and it is well documented that President Trump revered his father, Fred.

According to Hurst, Walt Disney shared the same combination birth order.

I know this personality very well, as it is the personality of the boy I have already told you about, whom we have affectionately called "IncredaBO" since the day he was born, and joked that he is "destined for world domination." We laugh that keeping him humble is our toughest job. His siblings help a lot with that! I wonder if Fred and Mary ever joked about Donald like that. I wonder if his siblings helped to keep him humble. Thank goodness the double birth order also creates a compassionate, loving, and giving person!

By their fruits you shall know them

President Trump's psychology also comes into play when you see his own children. Since he seems to have been well parented, even through his divorces (which often accompany a life of excess and access), he prioritized his children. Ivanka talks about sitting in his office constructing skyscrapers with Legos. All of the children talk about their father's working hard to teach them the ropes of business and how to value money.

It is interesting that President Trump has the same number of children as his own parents, and Donald Trump Jr. (despite his own divorce) has five children of his own. When I had my fifth child, someone told me that is the number of grace. I have never found that documented in scripture, but I do find it interesting that children from families of five tend to have distinct and interesting lives.

I operate largely on faith, and often I lead with prayer. This presidential race was no exception. Every time I began to pray about and reflect on Donald Trump, the same still, small voice repeated this thought to me: "You will know them by their fruits."

At first I was confused by that thought. I knew about Donald Trump's divorces, the wives, the casinos, the reality show...none of that spoke to my spirit in ways I liked on a surface level. So why did this thought keep coming to me? What did it have to do with my prayer about whom to support for president?

So I did what I do in such dilemmas—I went to God's Word, and I read the chapter and verse:

> "Ye shall know them by their fruits. Do men gather grapes of thorns, or figs of thistles? Even so every good tree bringeth forth good fruit; but a corrupt tree bringeth forth evil fruit. A good tree cannot bring forth evil fruit, neither can a corrupt tree bring forth good fruit. Every tree that bringeth not forth good fruit is hewn down, and cast into the fire. Wherefore by their fruits ye shall know them." (Matthew 7:16–20 KJV)

Then I began watching the children of the candidates, instead of the candidates themselves. I was awed and captivated by the Trump children and grandchildren—the fruit. And as I watched, I was less awed by those whose values matched mine more closely, that were bashing Donald Trump for being Donald Trump.

The Loudon household's unofficial motto is "Let's remember, everyone thinks we're a nice, normal family." Believe me, I wasn't judging. I was trying to see who had really invested in his children in outstanding ways.

My own five children vary from day to day. I differ with some of their choices, but I hope that my dedication to them will show up as they mature into adulthood. So I couldn't help but notice the competence and grace of the Trump children, which I now know extends to their spouses and their children.

Knowing this man *by his fruit* began to make some sense to me. Now that I have a much more personal knowledge of their family, I am only more impressed with what they are all willing to sacrifice for the good of our country. I am impressed with their deep loyalty to one another, even through divorce and all the complications of life. The bond between those who have loved this president is amazing and truly telling. Now that I know them much more personally, I am only more impressed.

It's tough to leave a legacy to so many grandchildren, and the president is already on quite a roll! He had eight grandchildren when he ran, with Eric and Lara, now my friends, giving birth to little Luke not long after the inauguration! But I believe that is what keeps the work of the president motivating and meaningful to him. I believe his life's work to this point is to leave a loving and happy legacy to his grandchildren, regardless of the personal cost to him. This would be typical of the self-actualized, double birth order, fourth and first child in the final chapter of his life—he would want to take on a great, final challenge, but he would want to use his unabashed leadership abilities to do it. In this case, I believe, this is the ultimate gift a human being can give.

To be able to complete life reaching goals and personal contentment is the self-actualization that Abraham Maslow spoke of in his famous "Hierarchy of Needs." I believe the forty-fifth president of the United States has achieved the highest Maslovian level, and perhaps higher, if there is such a thing.

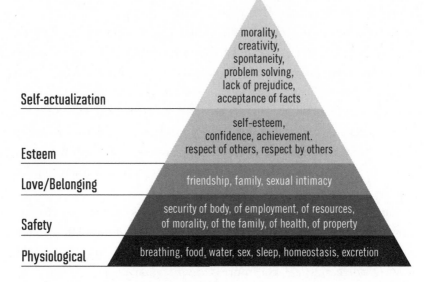

As it is sung in *Les Misérables*, my favorite musical, "to love another person is to see the face of God." I believe that this president has come to his Maslovian self-actualization, and his sense of faith, and family, and that his single vision for the rest of his life is to leave a legacy of love, life, and yes, fun!

But why does he tweet?

I believe there are four reasons Donald Trump tweets. One, he loves fun, as the natural birth order of the fourth of five dictates. Sometimes, he uses his tweets to be funny. I have to admit that about 25 percent of the time I laugh out loud when I read his tweets. I know they will send the regressive left into a frenzy, the Never-Trumpers will still be unable to understand, and he will have all of his enemies saying ridiculous things that are, indeed, amusing to those of us watching. So he uses tweets effectively for comedic effect.

Two, he uses his tweets to validate his base and the American people. This is part of his charitable nature. He knows that the American people are frustrated, most of all because they feel they haven't been heard by politicians and their ideas never make it to media. They think politicians don't listen. President Trump's tweets won him the support of countless voters who recognized in them the thoughts and feelings they thought no one heard. But President Trump's tweets today win him the most loyal base in American political history.

Three, his tweets are part of his chess match with his enemies. He knows he can tweet a blanket statement and get his enemies speculating about what he really means. The establishment evaluates tweets based on convention and the advice of consultants. But President Trump defies those things. Coolly playing his long game, he usually gets the reaction he wants.

And I have to admit, I do the same thing. About a quarter of the time, when the president sends out his first tweet of the day, I rate it according to the apoplexy it induces among his enemies. If they really, really hate it, and their heads are spinning, I understand that it is probably a good idea. Their disdain for him is often feigned outrage, not because they are outraged by what he has said or done, but because they have realized that, once again, they are losing, and can't seem to catch a break.

I think the president also tweets to test the waters with his base. That's what he did during the campaign when he proposed tariffs to equalize the trade war on America.

I oppose tariffs. I never met a tax I liked, and I don't like them for anyone else, either. But when I saw how loony the left went when the president mentioned tariffs on steel and aluminum, I knew I had to be missing something. Looking deeper, I realized that we didn't need to fear a trade war—we were *already* in a trade war. I understood the patriotic argument the president was making. I asked Fox audiences, "How come it isn't a trade war when the United States is being disproportionately taxed, but when the United States wants to level the playing field, suddenly we are on the brink of a trade war?" Sure enough, Trump's base understood. They wanted to stand with him against the accusations of the left. He used those tweets for testing.

About a quarter of the time, the president does seem to use his tweets for policy. He talks about the regulations he is loosening to help

American business, or improvements in medical care for our veterans. These are basic policy tweets that any president would make, but the media still haven't caught on to that reality.

The psychology of the Never-Trumpers, and how little they matter to the president's success

A friend of mine once told me that he sees his enemies as orange cones he has to steer around to get where he wants to go. After all, he says, it is more entertaining to look at enemies with orange traffic cones on their heads.

I try that, but sometimes I simply see demon heads instead. The traffic cone vision doesn't always do it for me.

I don't know how the president thinks of his enemies, but I would make a bet he has a mental map he uses to steer around his enemies and naysayers. But no matter how he handles his enemies, I think I do know how he views the Never-Trump crowd.

Convention. Convention. Convention.

There are few things more stifling to creative producers like Trump than those who see everything through the lens of convention. "That's the way we do it, yessireee!" only makes those creative, driving personalities want to shake someone and yell, "Noooooooooo!"

There is nothing more threatening to a conventionalist than an attack on his tidy little mental files. And to a fun-loving creative genius, there is no bigger buzzkill than a conventionalist. They will always be at odds.

To be sure, there are Never-Trumpers who are merely jealous Swamp Monsters. There are establishment elitists who have evil intent. But there are also Never-Trumpers who simply like the solid lines of traditional republican governance and don't want anyone to upset the apple cart. Then along comes Trump, a declared disrupter who wants to dismantle the traditional apparatus and build it better. No wonder the two sides don't see eye to eye.

But it doesn't really matter. Trump will steer around them and build his tower. He always has. They would be smart to get out of the middle of the road.

What type of Trump?

Perhaps the most compelling predictor of future behavior is that of personality type. I have long been a student of these inventories, and one of the first things I ask people I am really interested in knowing is their type. Maybe one day I will write a book on all the famous people I know and their types, because I find it fascinating.

I don't know the president's personality type, but I'd love to. Some things about it seem particularly noticeable. So here we go...

According to the Myers-Briggs organization, there are sixteen personality types formed by four basic characteristics, or *continua*, as they're called. That sounds complicated, but if you know someone well, it's quite simple to guess his or her type pretty closely. Here is how they break it down:

Favorite world: Do you prefer to focus on the outer world or on your own inner world? This is called Extraversion (E) or Introversion (I).

Information: Do you prefer to focus on the basic information you take in or do you prefer to interpret and add meaning? This is called Sensing (S) or Intuition (N).

Decisions: When making decisions, do you prefer first to look at logic and consistency or first look at the people and special circumstances? This is called Thinking (T) or Feeling (F).

Structure: In dealing with the outside world, do you prefer for things to be decided, or do you prefer to stay open to new information and options? This is called Judging (J) or Perceiving (P).

Extroversion vs. Introversion

The first of the four continua may be the easiest to determine. President Trump obviously gets his energy from people, as we know from his rallies, and leads an active social life. He is almost certainly an extrovert. So we can proceed from there.

Sensing vs. Intuition

My best guess is that our president is an intuitor. He often bucks conventional wisdom and seems to rely on his gut. Good intuitors know when to rely on their instinct and when to base judgments on simple, sensory data. The president wouldn't be so wildly successful if his intuition didn't give him a leg up in business and in life.

But... Feels...

The thinking vs. feeling continuum is slightly less defined but still interesting to consider. The president certainly leads with his heart, as we see over and over. We saw this when he brought the Angel Moms (mothers who have lost children to illegal aliens) to his rally, when he held the "listening session" with the students in the Florida school shooting in 2018, and when he paused to listen to the heart of the College of the Ozarks cafeteria worker who cried as she thanked him for her two-hundred-dollar bonus.

He undeniably leads with his heart, but I don't think he lets the emotion dictate how he implements that leadership. I think that unlike most in media and on the left (and frankly, even some on the right), the president knows when to lead with emotion and when to lead with solid data.

He changed his mind on abortion, knowing he would pay a price for going from "pro-choice" to pro-life, but he did it when he witnessed a close friend struggling to keep a baby alive in the womb.

That might seem to indicate an emotional or "feeling" basis for his decision.

But he also changed his mind on the Second Amendment. From an emotional perspective, it is easy to say the answer to violence is to ban all guns. But when you look at the data, the irrationality of banning guns quickly becomes apparent. The logic of gun confiscation would require us to ban cars, which kill more children than guns. More people die where fewer guns are in the hands of good people. And only law-abiding people would abide by more gun laws, anyway. "Just ban guns" isn't such a logical position after all.

When I was in college, I supported a gun ban. It wasn't until I became a researcher and learned to rely on data, not feelings, that I changed my mind.

The president changed his mind too, and in both these cases, he chose the side that is harder for a public figure to hold. This tells me his decisions were rational, or *thinking*, and that the president trusts his own ability to evaluate data and make solid choices.

While the president is certainly empathic, he also knows to use calculations based upon solid data for public policy. That is the kind of strength and presence of mind America needs in a president. That is why an intuitive America elected this president, even if most people don't realize it.

Don't be so judgy!

If we all had a dime for every time a snowflake utters that slogan, we would all be as rich as Trump!

But we have to make judgements every day in our lives, and the snowflakes of the world could use a stiff dose of better judgment.

This is the murkiest of the four continua with regard to the president, but my guess is that he is close to the middle of this continuum. I think he probably vacillates between judging and perceiving. Here's why.

President Trump is obviously decisive. I imagine that when he was young, he would have tested decidedly in the judging category. But I think as he grew older, and through his sophisticated ability to realize his own mistakes and what doesn't work, he may have grown more perceptive.

Despite his decision-making abilities and strong leadership skills, I believe that in recent years, the president has kept his mind open to the possibility that he could be wrong, and I think that is why he likes to listen to opposing views.

I see this category as perhaps his strongest asset as president. He's decisive, but open to differing opinions. Still, I would put him leaning J, because he seems to believe in some absolute, foundational truths, that aren't open to perceptions.

The Total Presidential Package

This combination, if my analysis is on point, would make the President an ENTJ. Here is what the 16 Personalities.com site says that would mean:

> "The Commander" (16Personalities.com): ENTJs are natural-born leaders. People with this personality type embody the gifts of charisma and confidence, and project authority in a way that draws crowds together behind a common goal. But unlike their Feeling (F) counterpart, ENTJs are characterized by an often ruthless level of rationality, using their drive, determination and sharp minds to achieve whatever end they've set for themselves. Perhaps it is best that they make up only three percent of the population, lest they overwhelm the more timid and sensitive personality types that make up much of the rest of the world – but we have ENTJs to thank for many of the businesses and institutions we take for granted every day.

Other interesting ENTJ's are thought to be Margaret Thatcher, Bill Gates, Aristotle, Alexander Hamilton, Karl Rove, Dick Cheney, Al Gore, Nancy Pelosi, Bernie Sanders, Jim Carrey, FDR, David Petraeus, Whoopi Goldberg, David Letterman, and finally, me.

Wouldn't that explain a lot? If weaker, timid personality types that make up the world are naturally "overwhelmed" by the ENTJ, we can see why the vitriol of some persists against our President.

I think we have to ask ourselves what Personality type we would want as leader of the Free World. What traits would we prefer for someone to stand up to dictators and those who have corrupted our federal agencies?

Frankly, I didn't know what I would discover as I began this theoretical analysis of our President's personality, but I can honestly say I was pleasantly surprised with what I found out. It may sound self-aggrandizing for me to say, since I share this type, but if he is an ENTJ, I really believe our country is well-served. I can't think of a stronger leader than one who leads with his heart, decides with his head, and knows how to attain the goals he sets forth. The ENTJ has *mad* presidential skills!

If the establishment could ever open its eyes and see the true psychology of this president, who has lived a life and integrated its lessons into his leadership style, I think they could relax in his mental fitness, and even mental prowess. Dare I say that this president has perhaps the greatest mental stability in recent history, because with all the haters out there, it takes great courage and yes, as he says himself, "STA-MIN-A" to lead this country!

CHAPTER 11

THE PATH BACK TO SANITY

How to Stay Sane When Even the Experts Want You Crazy

"Come unto me, all ye that labour and are heavy laden, and I will give you rest."
—Matthew 11:28 (KJV)

People often ask me how to "de-stress." To some, that sounds "snow-flakey," but in the current political climate, we have observed some people losing it, if only momentarily, because of political conflict.

Remember those people wailing at President Trump's inauguration?

There are many theories out there, but I have learned through counseling many people and watching them try different methods that there are some effective ways to get through times of stress, and almost none of them are ones you will read about in *Cosmo* magazine or other purveyors of pop-psych advice.

I have learned that so much of life is counterintuitive. That shouldn't surprise us, because God Himself is the ultimate irony. I love how He loves to dwell in the realm of irony. I teach my children to watch for it, to listen to that still, small voice that explains all of this if only we will be still and know that He is God.

He explains it all in the irony cited all over the Bible, from its very premise.

He could have just reigned, but instead he chose to give us free will. He could have come with thunder on a white horse with all splendor and glory, but He chose instead to come humbly, in an animal barn, with a feed trough for a crib. Can you imagine?

So why are we surprised when He uses the simple to once again confound the wise? He said He would!

The onslaught of Fake News is contributing to all the stress, but it has had the unintended benefit of forcing us to take a critical look at the news, which we might have taken at face value in days gone by.

But even if we know that most of the conventional wisdom on staying sane is Fake News, that doesn't answer what really *does* work.

I submit that God's simple promises are an easy road map to sanity. I don't know why we tend to look everywhere except there, but we do. I do. But after a lifetime of researching this, I have found that God's principles actually work to maintain sanity in a mad world.

- Focus on others, not yourself.
- Ignore worldly, trendy advice about staying sane and stress-free.
- Man is meant to be free. That applies to economies, too. The freer we are, the saner we are. We must support politicians who understand that.
- The mind-body concept is clearly laid out in the Bible. Read it. It can make all the difference.
- Fasting, prayer, freedom, helping others, and loving your neighbor may provide the perfect path to sanity, and health!

The "Take Time for You" Myth

"A generous person will prosper; whoever refreshes others will be refreshed."

—Proverbs 11:25 (NIV)

"Take time for you" is probably one of the most dangerous, stress-inducing statements of all time. It doesn't work. In fact, most "depressed" people, I have found, take a *lot* of time for themselves, and that is much of the problem.

Think about it. Of those you know, who is the most mentally healthy and happy? The friend who has regular spa days and shopping sprees, with vacations and clothes and a cleaning lady, or the friend who knows a good day's work, whose hands are calloused, who works out, and does for others?

Now don't get me wrong—there are certain moments in life when only a new pair of shoes will help! But if your basic coping strategy is pampering yourself, you are probably among those who believe they are "depressed." My fellow psychologists go nuts when I say it, but I have tested it, and it is true.

Many of my famous friends come to me for advice since they can never really trust others in my profession. I don't charge them, and I tell them I am speaking as their friend, not their therapist, but I still offer the best advice I can. And when my friends tell me they feel "depressed," I have them take two days (a weekend is perfect) and try an experiment.

The first day, it's all self-indulgence. That is, after all, what every magazine and meme advises, right? I tell them, "Treat yourself! Go to a spa, get a makeover, do yoga or meditation, eat your favorite food, buy yourself a present. Do whatever you have always been told will make you feel nurtured."

But on the second day, I tell them, do something completely different: "Spend the day fasting and serving others, take a risk and make yourself uncomfortable, give away something you're deeply attached to." This is a tall order, and not everyone completes it, but those who do have better results. Because it's simply a fact that those who do for others rather than themselves tend to be happier and feel less stressed.

Now, there is such a thing as clinical depression, which is a chemical problem, and when you see it, you know it. These people cannot function. They can't work, they have trouble sleeping and eating, they may be substance-dependent, and they may have thoughts of suicide.

We all have down days, but true depression is not circumstantial. In other words, it is not caused by bad days, bad news, or even bad relationships. Depression is constant and all-consuming, and a truly depressed person cannot snap out of it if his lover comes back, he wins the lottery, or he gets the job he always wanted. His brain chemistry is off balance, and he requires intense therapy and usually medication or some natural intervention to restore the balance.

Many people think they are depressed because a therapist told them they are. Therapists, in turn, are under enormous pressure to give a diagnosis, which is required for the patient to be reimbursed for his therapy by his insurance carrier or the government. Depression is one of the most innocuous-sounding diagnoses, so the therapist writes it down on the form. It's a faulty system in so many ways. Much of what medical and therapeutic professionals do is for the sole purpose of avoiding a lawsuit. Frivolous diagnoses are no exception, sadly. But the implications can be terribly damaging to the patient, who now feels labeled and stuck in his diagnosis identity.

A cynic would point out that this is a business that relies on repeat customers. If you don't think you have a reason to come back for more therapy, you might not make the effort. If clients don't return, psych businesses don't thrive. This is an unmentionable truth in my profession.

So, as in every aspect of life these days, we have to be our own researchers, our own critical thinkers, and, in too many ways, our own doctors.

UnitedHealth Group released a study on the health benefits of volunteering that found that people are mentally and physically healthier when they volunteer. Seventy-eight percent were said to have lower stress levels because of volunteering.[1] Keep in mind that this report is from a health insurance company, which wants to keep its costs down by promoting the wellness of its customers. There is nothing in the report that encourages people to pamper themselves. It's all about doing for others.

On my worst days, I visit a nursing home and just love on the people there. My mom was a director of nursing, so I feel at home there, and I always leave in a great mood. I used to visit homeless animal shelters, but when we ended up with a dozen adopted pets, I realized that may not have been my most productive service activity.

The best therapy I know is doing for others. Try it!

But the news gets even better!

"Therefore, if you died with Christ from the basic principles of the world, why, as though living in the world, do you subject yourselves to regulations—"Do not touch, do not taste, do not handle," which all concern things which perish with the using—according to the commandments and doctrines of men?"

—Colossians 2:20–22 (NKJV)

Short of a serious charity commitment, there are other options. A good walk can really be cleansing. A bike ride on a pretty day can completely lift your heart and soul! Now that the leftist elites at Michigan State have decided that yoga (I always hated the whole idea, anyway) is "racist" and "contribut[es] to White Supremacy and the Yoga Industrial Complex," (whatever that is), we are free at last from that ridiculously useless habit to pursue things that really work.[2]

They really want to tell us what to eat, too. But now that veganism has been shown to decrease IQ, we can move on to the intermittent fasting making waves in the diet world, but mentioned in the Bible long before it became the hot new trend![3] The Society for Neuroscience reports that the benefits of intermittent fasting go far beyond weight loss and improved digestion.[4] But brain health looks like a side benefit of fasting, in both human and animal studies.

Studies examined IER, a biological marker of memory and learning, and found that fasting enhances memory and even improves the growth of new neurons in the elderly. IER can help patients recover from traumatic brain injury and stroke, and new studies suggest that fasting can even help prevent Alzheimer's and other neurodegenerative diseases. Some of the most promising work is showing that fasting can improve cognitive function and quality of life in those already diagnosed with these diseases. That puts fasting in the miraculous category. Jesus tried to tell us, but sometimes we are slow learners. So much for yoga and veganism!

But perhaps the most important benefit of fasting is what it does naturally to elevate hormones and brain chemistry that can prevent, lessen, and in some cases, even cure depression and anxiety disorders.

When you feel physically healthy, you will feel more mentally healthy, too. So fasting and praying are great tools for staying mentally sound in a mad, mad world! And it is all within your reach.

Look for what works for you. Give what you love to get. Serve where you love to be. Bless where you have been blessed. And watch your mood elevate organically, and know that you are one of the few who can crack the code on remaining sane in a crazy world.

What really eats at us

I have spent years asking people what they fear most that politics can influence. For years, the answer has been Islamic terrorism. And I have always noticed parallels between the modern fear of another Islamic terror attack and my own childhood fears of a nuclear attack.

As a child, I often went to bed trembling in fear that a nuclear bomb would drop that night. Similarly, I watched my own children fearing terror every day. As a mother, this infuriated me.

I loved Reagan for defending our country against the Evil Empire, allowing me to sleep at night. I believe that President Trump will likewise be credited for the defeat of ISIS and other terrorists. In Trump's first year in office, the number of terrorist cells in Iraq and Syria decreased from forty-five thousand to fewer than one thousand. According to US officials, nearly thirty-thousand coalition air strikes had killed more than seventy-thousand jihadists by 2017, and their numbers continue to decline.

The economy was another fear, but the economy took off and did well from the first day of Trump's administration. Even allowing for the expected free-market corrections of an unleashed economy, all economic indicators show that Trump's reduced regulation and pro-business policies are creating jobs and repatriating companies in droves. Economic fears, rampant under Obama and reflected in lowered consumer confidence and higher unemployment, were largely allayed with the new administration. But there was a new fear on the horizon.

It used to be terror that really ate at us, but President Trump changed that. Now, it is the chasm between those on the left and right.

We fear retaliation for our political beliefs. We fear being labeled. We fear losing our livelihoods because we support a certain political candidate. We fear being dehumanized by our political opponents.

Though the majority of polled Americans say they don't like divisiveness, the reality is that we don't do much to change it. Maybe that's because that is how our Founders set it up. They knew that the struggle between two strong political parties would tend to keep the pendulum centered, giving citizens on both sides representation and hearty debate.

But why is it that they seemed to be able to engage one another civilly, when it seems like we can't? I believe it is because we have systematically dehumanized those we disagree with, not only in our politics, but in life in general.

Anyone we perceive as a problem in our lives, we dehumanize.

We dehumanize babies that are inconvenient so that we can kill them. We spend $1.5 million of taxpayer money each day funding a private company to do it, so it feels cleaner to us. But it isn't clean. It's actually very dirty, and I would submit that the dehumanization we normalized in our culture in the 1970s has led us to a dangerous place today.

If it's a nuisance, kill it and call it abortion.

We have never before seen such a distinct dehumanization of our political enemies. The violence against anyone who supported Donald Trump has become rampant. Those who speak about tolerance are tolerant only of those who happen to agree with them. They dehumanize and harass those who do not.

As the left declines into a failing party, they attack more viciously. Even lawmakers on the left are calling for the harassment of innocent people on the right, simply for their political views. Livelihoods are attacked. Those who hold certain jobs are attacked. The media remain relatively silent.

It seems like those who are losing are clinging bitterly to blaming, and ultimately hating, to the point of dehumanization.

If it doesn't conveniently fit in your lifestyle, call it immoral or racist, and attack it for convicting you.

If it isn't something you understand, rather than study it, or face facts that don't fit in your preference, distract yourself with something else. Manufacture another crisis. Accuse another innocent. Point another finger. That gets easier every day.

If it doesn't fit in your worldview, ignore it, and listen to your own echo chamber instead.

The Seven Deadly Psychological Sins of Socialism

Every dictator worth his weaponry knows that to control people, you have to exploit the vulnerabilities in their mental processes to convince them that you aren't hurting them, but in fact, helping them.

This isn't easy, but for some people, it comes naturally. We see it in wife beaters. They convince the victim she isn't good enough or that she can't get anyone else to love her. Evil has a way of helping her believe the lie, so she submits to the abuse, perversely enough, to convince herself that she *is* lovable. Every psychologist knows that if you can convince the victim she is lovable, she can escape the prison of her own mind and leave her abuser.

It sounds so simple, but it isn't. And neither is helping those used and abused by politics. In some ways, it is even harder, because our tribal tendencies come into play. Governments convince large groups of people that they are victims who need the government to save them. Letting "Big Daddy" government save you is so much easier that "adulting," admitting you are wrong, and taking responsibility for your *own* life.

It is unpleasant to be confronted with an idea that is inconsistent our current beliefs—we call that cognitive dissonance—and our brains try to avoid such stress by quickly "putting away" the challenging idea. This can be done in various ways—avoidance, distraction, projection, accusation, blame, dismissal—and our society has plenty of cures for what ails us when we don't want to face truths that might force us to change.

But there is a basic human morality in our soul that makes us long for God, and in that longing, we also feel drawn to be more like Him, even when we don't know it. That means we are drawn to love people and want to be at peace with them, because that is God's nature—and therefore, that is our nature.

In times of war, for example, we intentionally dehumanize the enemy so that we can kill him with the least possible mental stress. Military brass spends years grooming soldiers to dehumanize the enemy.

I recently toured Israel and spent hours walking through museums that highlight the use of propaganda for dehumanization. It's heartbreaking and difficult to digest. We know this is how the socialists of the Third Reich committed the atrocities they did in World War II. They convinced their people that Jews were less than human. That made it easier for them to disconnect from the human side of us that wants to love people, and to carry out the maniacal wishes of a cruel, evil dictator.

The same thing has happened in every society whose elite who wanted to control the citizenry. Take Pol Pot, Mussolini, Lenin, Stalin, Castro...the list is endless. They had a few things in common. I call them the "Seven Deadly Sins of Psychological Socialism."

1. They are all leftists who grew the size and scope of their government to better control the people.
2. They believed they were smarter than everyone else and knew best how everyone should live his life.
3. They convinced their citizenry that the lovers of individual freedom (conservatives) were backward and evil.
4. They convinced their citizenry that they were victims who needed a savior (the government, their dictator).
5. They turned the government into a weapon against the people, while convincing the people these bureaucrats were their fierce defenders.

6. They convinced their citizenry to relinquish freedoms under the guise of protection.
7. They dehumanized the enemies of their control.

The North Korean government—which President Trump has handled with such mastery—controls all media so that its citizenry remains focused on military achievements and content with oppression. The government controls everything they eat and see. They are fed almost nothing, watch their loved ones starve or be tortured to death, and yet for the most part, they remain intensely loyal to the regime.

In their propaganda, they are told that the whole world is evil, and that their "Dear Leader" is merely trying to save them, while the world is trying to kill them. The only explanation for such a story, of course, is that the rest of the world is full of evil people, and only Kim Jong-un can save them.

It sounds extreme to us, because our Founders carefully put measures in place to protect our people from such disillusionment. But the Germans thought they did, too, after World War II; in fact, many of those very measures are responsible for the rapes and killings taking place daily as Islamic immigrants pour into the country. The elite in the European Union have convinced the citizenry that the concept of tolerance must go this far to protect them from the atrocities of Hitler—it must include tolerance for those who want to kill them.

Today, tens of thousands—or possibly millions—of militant Jihadists are invading Europe, while the elitist leaders there are inviting them in, turning their heads the other way while women are raped in the streets and citizens are dying. The similarities to World War II are haunting, and yet they have dehumanized anyone who doesn't agree with them to retain power and wealth.

We see it right here in our own country. When Barack Obama became president, we saw a lot of changes that mirror the Seven Deadly Sins I listed above:

1. Obama and his leftist-socialist cabal grew the size and scope of their government to better control the people.
2. Obama's administration knew best how Americans should live their lives.
3. They knew they had to convince their electorate that the political right in their country was backward and evil.
4. They knew they had to convince their electorate that they were victims who needed to be saved by Obama and an ever-enlarging government.
5. They weaponized their government agencies to use them against their opponents and the American people, while convincing their voters that they were their fierce defenders.
6. They knew they had to convince their citizenry to relinquish their freedoms under the guise of protection, using every crisis to expand their own power.
7. They dehumanized any and all enemies of their control, thus enabling them to excoriate them at every turn with zero reprisal by their base.

Am I comparing Obama to Hitler or other monstrous dictators? Of course not. I am simply pointing to tactics employed by today's political elite. You can draw your own conclusions.

So what can we do?

This is tough. If someone is trying to subvert our Constitution and run our republic like a dictator, that is enraging. If someone is even letting it gently slide that direction for his own political power, that is still enraging.

Fortunately for those of us who understand freedom and faith, the answers are not only constant, but timeless.

We are called to love.

It sounds trite, but trite indicates simplicity, and this call is anything but simple.

There are volumes of books on how to love the unlovable, but for me, I have found humility to be the key. I try to remember how many times in my life I have been wrong. This isn't to diminish my own confidence or abilities, but only to check my ego at the door so I can deal with everyone on the same level.

During the Trump campaign, for more than one year, when I spoke to audiences around the country, my speech was "Have You Ever Been Wrong?" I mentioned this in Chapter 2. But I think it is important to note that if we are to make a difference in the hearts and mind of those who have bought into the Seven Deadly Sins of Socialism, we aren't going to get there by preaching to our own choir. We have to get in there, to love, to find what we agree about, and to be compassionate.

Loving the Unlovable

It's possible. I promise. I have proved this in my life, and you probably have too, though you may not realize what you did or how to replicate it.

We will get into it more in the next chapter, too, because there are "tricks," so to speak, and ways to use the tools God has given you that are unique to you. That's the fun part!

Generally speaking, though, it is critical to start from a place of humility and an openness to learning from the person you think is wrong.

The difference between conservatives and liberals is the reason most of us are pretty convinced we are right. It is this: Most conservatives have been liberals once upon a time. That makes us feel like we are coming from a place of wisdom, because we used to think like most of the liberals we try to talk to.

It's a little like talking to a child who just hasn't had a chance to learn yet, if we can think of it that way.

Come unto me like a little child…

Jesus says, "Truly I tell you, unless you change and become like little children, you will never enter the kingdom of heaven" (Matthew 18:3 NIV).

Our adopted son, Samuel, who has Down syndrome, pulled a pan of hot grease off the stove because he wanted the fries my husband was cooking. He didn't know that he couldn't simply pull the pan down to get some. He didn't understand how hot the pan was, or that he would end up in the Children's Hospital clinging to life in a burn unit for weeks. He didn't weigh the skin grafts and pain before grabbing the pan of fries.

There was no way he could have understood how this accident, which happened while I was out of town, would challenge our marriage. He couldn't understand how, as parents, we blame ourselves for such a tragedy. He couldn't have known that long after he recovered, our other children would still come to me in the night in a pool of tears remembering the screams, the helplessness, and the guilt for not watching him more closely. He couldn't have known the fear that would paralyze us in many ways after that day.

I am convinced that Samuel made us better parents and a closer-knit family that day, but not for the reasons you might think.

Parents and children are often challenged by the push and pull of the "you have"—"I want"—"why can't I have it/do it/ know it"—and the ever-present "because I said so" moments in life.

My family is no exception. But when I look back on that horrible day that took so much from our family, I realize the profound lesson my children learned: You can't explain to a baby why he can't have the fries in the hot pan of oil.

Countless times, and still today in their teen years, I have taken them back to that day.

"Why can't I go with my friends to a movie?" Remember Samuel with the hot pan, and how even if you tried, you couldn't have explained how you knew it would hurt him, and that even though he wanted those fries so badly, it wouldn't be worth it in the long run? Do you think he would have listened or believed you if you tried to tell him?

Not a chance.

You can't impart wisdom. Not really. I do believe that reading the Word of God brings a supernatural wisdom that surpasses our human ability to understand, but only God can do that. As mere mortals, even really loving and wise parents or older siblings, we simply can't.

Did you ever notice that the more wisdom you think you have and the more you wish you could impose it on your children, the less likely they are to listen?

Part of that is certainly our sinful nature and our constant need for Christ. But the rest of it is because we learn by doing. About the only teaching we can do by talking is using someone's own experiences as a springboard and helping him see how he can find meaning in his own way.

Just as my children have ever since the day Samuel pulled the pan off the stove.

They tried to tell him not to do it. We had all told him dozens of times not to touch anything on, around, or near the stove. We were always careful to turn pot handles in so he couldn't accidentally pull one down. This was all to no avail.

If my theory is true—that most conservatives used to be liberals and most liberals have never been conservatives—then the analogy between parent and child works, too.

Most parents remember being children, but no child has the wisdom of already experiencing adulthood. So you simply can't expect him to have the wisdom of someone with that experience.

But somehow, sometimes, our children do listen to us, even without having experienced adulthood. Why is that?

It is when we approach them in love and help them find their own solutions.

When my older children want to do things that I know could hurt them, I draw on that day with Samuel and the ways we all knew it would hurt him, tried to warn him, but he was blinded by his love of fries.

Find common ground with the people you think have an openness to understanding the truth as you see it about politics, and that is your entry! Maybe you agree on love of animals, or peace in the Middle East. Whatever it is, find it, and start there.

Get that person to run through in his mind how he decided that, and see his own road map to the next smart decision. His own map is all he has. Teach him to read it in a new way, and he can go places on his own.

I love to tell the story of Xander.

He saw me on a reality show where I was portrayed as a judgmental, right-wing, religious zealot. You know, like we all are told we are every day.

Xander was a left-wing gay man who had a show in New York and an audience composed mostly of gay and transvestite people, but he was a believer.

He attacked me on Twitter for being a fake Christian.

I responded in love, because there was something in his tweet that told me he was searching, asking a question, more than pointing a finger. That began a dialogue that he will tell you led to his political and spiritual conversion.

By the time the presidential election rolled around, Xander was one of candidate Trump's best advocates in the most unlikely crevices of the electorate. That holds to this day, where Xander now tells his own conversion stories! It's amazing what can begin when the simple rules of respect, humility, civil discourse, and love enter into the rancor that is usually politics.

If you don't win people over to your view, at least you know that you listened, loved, and perhaps planted a seed that may sprout one day when you least expect it.

That's madly awesome!

CHAPTER 12

STICKS AND STONES

The Greatest Lessons for the Path to Success for our Children, and Ourselves

"Making the decision to have a child—it is momentous. It is to decide forever to have your heart go walking around outside your body."

—Elizabeth Stone[1]

If I could give you a piece of advice that would change your life, making you happier and more successful, would you take it?

I know you think you would, but you probably wouldn't. Most of us wouldn't. Have you ever stopped to realize how often we don't take solid advice, to our own peril?

Recently, my fifteen-year-old son, Jack, experienced his first heartbreak. It won't be his last. That's life.

He has watched his two older sisters grow, so he knows that girls are "crazy" from about fifteen to eighteen in a lot of ways. Boys can be, too, but my point of emphasis with him was that he would be smart to wait to go for girls until he is at marriage age. This whole ridiculous marriage rehearsal teenagers go through is so fruitless. But I did it. Most of us did it. And we lost a lot of time and self-confidence in the process. What a waste.

I'm a self-disciplined person who takes pride in her ability to forgo earthly pleasures to keep her eye on the prize, but it drives me mad that I sometimes just don't listen to wisdom. But why?

As a conservative, I think sometimes that I am allergic to waste, fraud, and abuse. Maybe that's why I can't stand to see people waste a moment of productivity making their own mistakes.

It's not pretty. It's not honorable. People look rather stupid when they make their own mistakes, and I don't really see our romance with such a colossal part of our culture that really gets us nowhere.

Statistically, when a young person dates before the age of twenty, there is about a 1 percent chance that he will actually marry the person he's dating and create a life with her.

So why do we go through this song and dance that only distracts us from so much mental steadiness and productivity?

The answer? For the same reason we do most things in our lives: We don't take advice from others. We have some sort of romantic fantasy about the idea of learning for ourselves.

But here is what I have learned in my study of people: The most successful people in life not only can, but *do* manage to take advice from others without learning the hard way.

We have a bizarre fascination and an unfounded respect for "learning things the hard way" and "letting people find out for themselves," but why? Maybe if we didn't, we would be not only more successful and productive, but happier? Failing isn't pleasant. So why add extra failure to the hard knocks that life already brings?

Much of this book has been about the mistakes people make and how to avoid them, or to help them to avoid them. Why not begin with one easy one? Take the advice of those you know and trust to be smart or successful in the arenas you wish to contend.

Since I moved to The Palm Beaches, after Governor Brown's actions forced us to leave California, I have learned more than ever. I joke that I am the youngest and poorest person at every social event I go to here! Everyone seems to be older than I, and everyone seems to be richer than

I. It's a fascinating culture, and so rich in wisdom. Rumor has it that Palm Beach is home to more billionaires than Monte Carlo. I don't know if that's true, but the fact is that billionaires are a different breed. Who knows if it a chicken or an egg that made it that way, but they are different. And they are different in some ways that surprise me.

Many of us think that billionaires are not great people, that they must somehow be greedy or self-indulgent. I have learned a lot from my friends here who have been wildly successful at what they do. I am a natural interviewer, so I have asked a lot of questions, and there are three profound differences I find in my successful friends when I ask:

- They soak up information from people they deem wiser than they.
- They do not find it necessary to make their own mistakes as readily.
- Failure simply does not impede subsequent efforts to succeed.

I have one friend, Tim Gannon, who is famous as the originator of the Bloomin' Onion, an appetizer dish consisting of one large onion cut to resemble a flower. He owns Outback Steakhouse, PDQ, Bolay, and probably more, but I have never asked. It doesn't matter. The first time we went out as couples with him and a friend, he took my little boys on a ride in his Lamborghini. That gave me the opportunity to talk to my boys about success, how Tim achieved success, and what makes a life "successful."

Tim's natural ability to blow businesses sky high and make his mark in his industry is amazing. But his psychology may hold the key to understanding why some people succeed and others don't, as well as the reason some people understand what makes successful government and others don't.

When he was young, like every young person, he had big dreams. He loved polo, and he wanted to play polo more than anything in the world.

He talked to a friend of his who was much older, wealthier, and wiser, and asked him how he could play polo. His friend told him that there were three ways:

- Marry well. Marry very, very well. Polo is expensive, and he knew Tim would need lots of money.
- Borrow money.
- The last way was to work hard at whatever he could do to be tremendously successful, and play later, after he made his money.

All of the thoughts must have filed through Tim's mind. Younger polo players have time to win championships, maybe even play with royalty, and go to the top of their field. Would he have time for all he wanted to accomplish in the sport that he loved if he waited until he went from rags to riches?

Without parents around to guide him, Tim knew instinctively he had to listen to the wisdom of his elders. He chose the hardest option, number three.

Tim's Bloomin' Onion generated a billion dollars in revenue, and at age forty-one, he started playing polo competitively. His team went on to win five U.S. Open championships by the time he was fifty.

Tim's story is one that I have heard over and over from my friends who are self-made and have accumulated ridiculous wealth. The common thread running through their stories is that they listened to the wisdom around them, and they followed it.

If I were a rich man...

I really thought I knew a lot about life and faith before I went to Israel. But Israel isn't something that someone can describe to you.

"Life changing."

Everyone uses those words when he returns from Israel. Just to give you an idea, one of my major political views changed completely. But *everything* changed to some degree. I am spiritually, politically, cultur-ally, intellectually, and faithfully better than I was before.

It's hard to describe the debt of gratitude I feel for the people who built the very faith that my own faith is built upon.

To walk where Jesus walked, to see the places He died and rose, to understand ancient and current struggles, to witness enemies striving to respect one another, to experience *real* security that we don't even know here in the United States, to touch the Western Wall by the Holy of Holies, to look up and see the enemy face to face and yet to know Who wins in the end, to see the desert where He fasted, touch the river where He was baptized, walk the streets he walked, to fall in love with the faith of my Savior, Jesus Christ…All I can is, you must go.

I couldn't meet an Israeli who didn't pull me aside and ask me to thank our president for all he has done.

I was completely, utterly changed.

What struck me again, though, was the success of Israel.

I was always the kind of person who had some sort of guilt for suc-cess. When my agent told me to use my "Doctor" title, I felt awkward about it, even though I had spent years and thousands of dollars to attain it. My family drove nice cars in my small town, and I felt bad for the kids whose parents couldn't drive nice cars. Maybe that's where it started.

But then Donald Trump walked out on that stage and said, "I want all of you to be as rich as me."

He wanted *all* Americans to be as rich as he.

I realized in that moment that my numerous socialist professors must have rubbed off on me more than I knew—I never realized that everyone in America could be rich. But why not?

That is certainly the mindset of Israel. For two thousand years, the Jews were deprived of their homeland. Today, they stand as this tiny county surrounded by enemies, with almost zero natural resources such as land mass or oil, and yet in a short seventy years they have built one the world's largest and strongest economies. Their military is one of the most formidable on earth. They give more to charity than any country besides the United States. And they have created the "Iron Dome" to protect them from the constant shelling of enemy fire. They have achieved massive success from almost nothing.

How?

When you watch what they have done, they have avoided the mistakes of other nations who have fallen, and they have emulated (and listened to the wisdom of) the United States.

How ironic is it that I needed to travel half way around the world to learn what another country learned about success from my own country! Thank you, Israel.

Why is it so hard for the left to learn?

But here comes another question: Why can't the left even learn the hard way from the mistakes they have made, especially in the last election?

In the 2016 election, Hillary Clinton was not a good candidate. Not only did she have a history of harassing the women her husband, former President Bill Clinton, abused, but she had some huge financial questions to answer regarding the Clinton Foundation, her dealings with Uranium One, her laziness on the campaign trail, and more. But the biggest problem for Hillary and the left was their lack of a platform.

The only thing they did consistently was divide—among racial, ethnic, gender, sex-preference, religious, age—or other lines. Identity politics was their mantra. The American people spoke loudly and said no.

The left lost soundly because of their identity politics, and yet when the race was over, there was never a regret from them. Later, as they began to look ahead to the 2018 midterms, into the 2020 election, and beyond, they continued the same platform: identity politics.

Their vitriol consumed them more and more, and they sank into a spiral of loss after loss until it appeared as if their entire party was one large echo chamber of losing, divisive, vitriolic identity politics.

I kept finding myself in the humorous position of trying to "help" the left out of the hole they had dug for themselves.

I truly believe we are all better with good competition. I long for days when we had a Democrat Party to polish us up with a little competition. But the Democrats have become blinded to the truth in every form. Their "Trump Derangement Syndrome" runs so deep that they can't find solid ground any more. The American public have watched in horror as the leaders of a once-solid party have devolved into ranting, screaming, dying hyenas.

This only grew their resentment of conservatives, and they began to act out against anyone who didn't believe what they believed. They undermined all civility by calling conservatives or anyone who voted for Trump Nazis, racists, homophobes, and more.

As I was contemplating the vitriol and intolerance of the left toward conservatives, I started to wonder if there is a fundamental difference between the psychological makeup of liberals and conservatives. And then it occurred to me...

Have you ever met a liberal who used to be a conservative? I have not. Maybe you have, but if you have, you can count them on one hand.

Have you ever met a conservative who used to be a liberal? I bet you have. I bet you have met many.

Most conservatives have been liberal. Most liberals have never been conservative.

Why is that significant?

As a student of developmental psychology, I find it phenomenal that there seems to be a fundamental difference in the arrival of our political beliefs. Conservatives usually get to conservatism by first being liberal. Liberals usually get to liberalism by being apolitical, or have always been liberal.

That fact is significant because it means that most conservatives have:

- Opened their minds to information contrary to what they currently believed.
- Listened to the wisdom of others.

- Been strong enough and had the confidence to consider changing their mind, even if it cost them popularity or friends.
- Admitted they were wrong before, and remained open to the possibility they could be wrong again.

How can you empathize with someone you cannot relate to? In other words, is a liberal even capable of considering your thoughts or feelings on an issue if he has never considered his own beliefs?

If you have never changed your mind because you learned something new, I would submit that you could believe your thoughts are infallible. Is that what keeps the liberals from learning and seeing truth?

The question is worth asking.

But what does that have to do with my original theory on billionaires?

Palm Beach is the home to perhaps the most famous billionaire in the world, Donald J. Trump. Everyone here has a story to tell because we all know the casual, relaxed side of the president.

I have picked up many stories from the president's friends about his profound graciousness, his unfathomable random acts of kindness, and his success.

The left says the president is the reason for their incivility. He's not. We on the right tried statesmanship (remember Dole, McCain, Romney, Bush...). Politicians failed us when they refused to stand and fight back. That's why Trump was such an appealing candidate to many of us—he's a fighter. He stands up to the bullies in Washington and in the media. We wanted that.

He didn't incite violence, and to confuse hitting back with inciting violence is dishonest.

Even Christ himself stood up to the tax collectors and pharisees in the Bible. I believe that part of the reason God gave us free will is to discern when to stand. President Trump, while being accused of madness throughout his presidency, has been able to withstand more hate and injustice daily than most of us endure in a lifetime. How is it that he seems to plow through life like a bulldozer and succeed over and over again? In his first year, it was calculated that he had one major success every thirty-six hours. And that was without the help of the spineless Republicans, the RINOs, the obstructionist Democrats, or the media. Somehow, he just succeeds.

My friend the Twitter phenom Bill Mitchell described the success of Trump as "muscle memory." Bill has a profound understanding of human behavior, probably because, unlike me, he didn't ever go to psych school!

Bill says that the reason Donald Trump proceeds with confidence, and seems to win as if he is anointed by God Himself is that he learns from the wisdom of others, and he operates on a success-producing "muscle memory."

We spoke about the importance of knowing we can be wrong. We talked about how the president describes many learning experiences that completely changed his mind on things that were closely held convictions once upon a time, such as abortion. But where does the importance of muscle memory come in, and why does it matter to the future of politics and success?

I believe he is God-ordained, at least in the ways I have described in this book. But he practices some things regularly that we can learn from too.

Going back to the four prerequisites a conservative had to go through to transform from liberalism to conservatism, if you have never opened your mind to information contrary to what you currently believe, is the muscle memory even there for someone on the left to seriously consider the opinions of someone on the left?

If after his public fight with Kim Jong-un, President Trump could humble himself and envision a way to forge denuclearization for the citizens he was elected to protect, can't conservatives and liberals find a way to work together? The left doesn't even know how much it could accomplish if it would at least work with conservatives on the things we can agree upon.

What if there is a deeper psychological reason that liberals can't open their minds and be more tolerant to conservatives?

What if there is an underlying fear of being wrong? What would prompt that? Is breakthrough even a possibility? Perhaps some people today are so lost they can't be helped. But we can still be there for those who want to learn, and answer their questions as honestly as we can. Perhaps more importantly, we can we raise our children to know their own possible error of opinions, listen to the wisdom of others, and have the confidence to proceed with a muscle memory of success.

Think about it.

If we can learn to *teach* those three things, we could not only avoid the pitfalls of getting through the teen years with our children (they might *listen* to us!), we could help them be set for success by helping them know what they don't know, listen to the wisdom of others, and commit their paths of success to muscle memory!

The Final Challenge: A Legacy of Civil Discourse

"Parenthood: It's about guiding the next generation, and forgiving the last."
—Peter Krause, actor

Supposing my theory about the left lacking the muscle memory of the success of transitioning into a new belief based upon wisdom gained through the experiences of others is correct, what do we do with that?

I know conservatives who dismiss leftists as junior high misfits who have a lifelong loser mentality that tribalizes them with those who are like them.

I have my moments, if I am honest, where I wonder if that is true. I have even seen some research that indicates it might be true, so take my advice here for what it is worth.

I believe we still need to enter with love and a goal of true civil discourse. I believe we still need to teach our children to lead with love. I believe my Grandma Lyda's theory that "Two Lips (and tulips) can tell...you get more bees with sweet honey pie!" And I believe that dismissing people, even when they are wrong, or misguided, is still selling our soul.

It is easy to dismiss the left as crazy, or angry, or rejects, or soulless.

I'm guilty too. My favorite quip of recent days comes from Brad Parscale, told me on our way to a rally for Trump, "You know, Trump always had the folks who showered before work. In 2016, he got the folks who showered after work. The Dems have those who don't shower at all!"

I honestly don't remember laughing that hard in ages. And every time I remember it, watching hysteria on TV or protestors at an event, I realize the accuracy, at least when I look at the loud few in pink hats screaming something about "the children"...and I laugh again.

We all have to find humor in our journey, but I really do believe we are the tolerant ones. We have the inside knowledge that we are not the judges of men's hearts, though we are often accused of being "judgy." We aren't. We can laugh and joke about the other side that doesn't seem to even want to understand us, but in reality, we are continuously searching for a way to help them see the truth we see. We want them on the winning side with us. We want to see America at her best ever, with us all united.

I believe that. I think if you look at Hollywood or sports, it is easy to see that they are intolerant to the point of being self-destructive and de-humanizing. You have to question the sanity of someone who clings so deeply to his intolerance of others' views.

But I think dismissing them is still wrong. I think doing hard things is often worth the cost. I believe that even if we never change a single mind or gain a single convert, we are stronger for it, we are better for it, and our children will learn the kind of grace that God gives us every day.

In *The Fountainhead*, Ayn Rand writes, "To sell your soul is the easiest thing in the world. That's what everybody does every hour of his life. If I asked you to keep your soul, would you understand why that's much harder?"

When my life is over, all I have ever wanted is for the Lord to say to me, "well done, good and faithful servant." I tell my children to put "She died tryin'" on my tombstone, because I will never stop trying. And I am happier for it.

On my recent trip to Israel, I realized there is a lot more to that than I could have ever known before I went there. But my trials and failures were each a tiny step in that direction. So even when we don't know what to do, we can do good, and we can be faithful. Being good and faithful are little steps toward the ultimate goal (the "Chief End" in the Westminster Catechism): To glorify God and to love Him forever.

Therefore, there is no effort wasted, no tear unwiped, no love unreceived.

God Himself says in Isaiah that His word does not come back void. Therefore, that which we do to love, even to the unlovable, will be returned rich with blessings. And this is true success.

My favorite musical is *Les Misérables*. I think about it so often because under Obama, I truly thought I would be one of those at the barricade taking my last stand for freedom and truth and righteousness. That is how I relate sometimes to the fear-mongering left who thinks the world is ending because Donald Trump is president. I felt that exact same way about Obama, but that was based on what I know to be true, based on trial and error and failure and success and all the things that come with learning, and being truly open to truth.

America was the closest it has ever been to ending under Obama. I believe that. I am so thankful that instead, for this moment anyway, a gracious God saw fit to give us the bloodless revolution through the most ironic and extraordinary of events, and the most unexplainable president in our history.

What is our burden for that? How do we thank Him for such grace when, as Pastor Curtis always reminded me, what we really deserve is hell and death?

As they sing in my favorite musical, "to love another person is to see the face of God."

So we have to love. And we have to contend. And we have to teach with a constant willingness to be taught. And we have to learn. And we have to fight.

In all my years and experience thus far, that is all I know to do. If for no other reason than to keep our sanity, and keep it well.

When I look back, I realize the journey to sanity in the midst of so much madness has been amazing! Knowing where I have come from, how much I have learned and been blessed, and how much I still have to learn and to bless, is inspiring every day! And continuing in that will always bring sunshine where there is rain, music where there is silence, and sanity where there is madness. Mad sanity. That's the truth as I know it, and I will always fight for Truth.

For our children, and our children's children, we can't relent. But we can enjoy the ride! I sure do!

As I used to close my radio shows: Go boldly now, and live the Truth. But in light of all the crazy, I will say it like this: Go *madly* now, and *fight* for truth! I am right here with you, each step of the way. To 2020, and beyond!

GRATITUDE
(in random order...)

I am thankful to those who joined me in the Donald J. Trump for President campaign when it felt like it was only us...your support meant everything to me, as I lost friends, business partners, clients, and even relatives over it. But the best part of it all was that we had each other, and now they wish they had been with us all along! That was an excruciatingly painful but beautifully refining way to learn who your real friends are. I will never forget you, and I am forever loyal for you having my back when I needed you most.

I am thankful to my Mar-a-Lago squad, who took me under their wing and welcomed my family. When the Governor of California forced our exit, you welcomed us with open arms, and changed everything I thought I knew about Florida, country clubs, and business. You support my passions, fill my life with sparkling beach days and starry white nights, and have become my refuge! Thank you!

I am thankful to our Palm Beach friends and business acquaintances who make it fun every day to live in this amazing city with all its charm, promise and adventure! I never dreamed I would, but I love my life here, and that is thanks to all of you!

I am thankful to my heart-of-gold publisher, Marji, my editors, Tom and Anne, and the team that makes up the Regnery reputation that made you my dream publisher before and during the entire process. It is an honor to publish with you.

To Sean Hannity, who has always believed in me, backed my work, taken my calls, trusted me with your microphone, and been my friend through sunny days and dark times, too. Your dedication to the election of this President and those of us who fought for him is unparalleled. #LNYHBT

To my right-hand guy, Producer extraordinaire, my Chupicabra, PV, Uncle Jason to my children, and one of the best business partners and critics someone who likes to win could ever have! Everyone who knows you knows you are the other half of my brain, my photographic memory, my spell check, the cattle prod pushing me forward and challenging me at every turn, my greatest frustration, my biggest fan, and the only person who could ever tolerate all of my drive and passion for my workaholic, ENTJ existence. You drive me nuts, keep me strong, challenge me non-stop, and know me better than I know myself. You brought me to this President that I so dearly love, and I am forever indebted.

To my husband John, MSJM, you are the best person I have ever known. You have never told me I couldn't accomplish every wild goal I have had, even when you knew they would cost you dearly. Whether I wanted to adopt a baby with Down Syndrome, run for the Senate, travel Europe, get my Ph.D., buy a boat, write a book, take in yet another orphaned animal or person, move to Alabama, or Cali, or Florida—you were always the same amount of excited as me! You have always been that solid, secure anchor in the stormy seas of life (many that I create all by myself), my rock, and the one constant that makes me feel brave enough to face every day with even more vigor! Making you my partner in life and work was the most rational and God-breathed choice I ever made. You are the father I hand selected for my children because I knew you would be the best daddy in the world and you SO are! You balance me in every way, and make me feel like I can conquer the world. Thank you for choosing me, loving me, praying for me, grounding me in Christ, tolerating my driven personality, giving me the world's five most amazing children, and the life of a princess, just like you promised me that very first day. I honestly never could have believed life could be as amazing as the one we have created together!

My sweet mama. Oh, how I wish I were writing this to you and you were here to read it. I miss you every moment of every day with all my heart, and I wish I could have been a better daughter to you. You raised me in every right way…to love Jesus, to give grace, to love animals, to be loyal, and fight fiercely when necessary. And you did it mostly as a single mom, alongside your anchor, Dale (I love you!) and your God! Aside from you living long enough to know all my children, I am so thankful that we agreed that Donald J. Trump should be our next President, my endorsement, and the one I defended on TV, while you were still here! I still learn from you every day, and in the oddest of ways, I think you teach me even more some days now than ever before. Thank you for being my mama forever! ONPN and I love you!

Daddy, thank you for teaching me how to love liberals, even when we disagree on practically everything. Thank you for teaching me to think critically, to be a research scientist, to always thirst for knowledge, to use my water and snow sports as my sanity, to study most when I think I know it all, to keep it simple when the distractions come, and for my ridiculously protracted education, I love you! Oh! And I almost forgot! Thank you for my ADHD! :)

To my friends, who have played an instrumental and inspirational role in this book, and in all that I am…Ang, Smexi & Kevi, Debbie "White Dove", Ola, Baby Beth, Kat, Em, my sisters…Susie and Kathy, Lara, Melanie, Porter, Angela, Brad, Sarah, Sean, Stephen, Dr. Matt Parker and Kelly, Ryan, Steve C., Andre and Papa, Dave and Stacy, JP, Scott and Renee, Mark L, Hal, KMC, Carrie S., Pastor Garlow, Susan, Melissa, Dr. Marc, Jack and Ann, Brian, Pam & Stan, The Ritters, Kate and HR, Dran, Francesca, Rabbi, Courtenay, Cynthia and fam, Cassandra, Alyssa, Barry, Julio, Eric, Mary Ellen, Terri, Linda C., Jennifer B., Kyle, Dr. Tess, Kristin, Jo Ann, George F., Kaya, Gayla, Melissa and Julie, Nelson, Thomas & Dr. Jim, Monica, Sly, Tito, Amanda, Iwona, Caroline, Rich & Jeannie,

Derek, Alex, John and Miranda, Rusty, Gene, Deanna, Chris, Dan, Steve, John, BJ, Michael, Laura, Jess, Harlan, John R., Jess, Tristan, Ashley, Morgan O., Dathan, Shaun, Dan & Nigel, Machelle, Nicole, Alex, Brad, Christl & Forrest, Jamey, Kelly, Georgann, Lisa & Greg, Jeff & Ann, Will, Landon, Steven, Peggy Jo, Ravi, Niel, Paula, Heather, Andrea, Andy, Gol, Lee and Erika, Mike, Sue, Zel, Rob, Mark and Amy, Tom & Daneen, Terrye, Eileen, Elisa, Foster, Chris, Kathy, Bubba, Ken and Aimee, Carrie, Michelle M., Dave, Steve, Mark, Marc, Courtney, Noelle, Tressie, Diamond and Silk, Hogan, Antony, Kayleigh, Dianna DLG, Diana, Donna and Woody, Bill, John, Ann, Lainie, Shannon, Xander, James & Sandy Jo, Mary Alice, Tim, Shante, Ali, Mercedes, Bev, Dr. Nina, Pete, Neil, Dana that I love and your whole, sweet fam, The American Women of Influence delegation to Israel...and so many more!

To my children...

My beautiful, capable, fearless, funny, quirky, graceful, sarcastic, soulful Lyda. You inspire me. You make life easy and so much richer and more fun to live! There is no one who makes me laugh harder, well up with pride, and want to be a better person, more than you. Thank you for that. It is an honor to be chosen and loved by you, the way you make me feel like I am always your Number One. The way you harness your uniqueness, and the way you counter the tide...you're my dream.

My Sweet Lily Love, my sweetest baby. I have never known anyone with such a sweet and simultaneously strong heart. You have taught me to love deeply, to relax more, to find solace in music, to worry less what the world thinks, and to be my creative self. I love the way you still protectively hold my arm when we walk together and still stop to love on me when you know I need it. I know there is not another soul alive who knows that. My tattoo partner...you are and always will be my little pocket full of sunshine! My perfect opposite, and yet my heart's other puzzle piece. Mwafoo Mwafoo!

Jack, you are full of surprises and abilities that I love discovering on the adventure of getting to be your mama! Your sweet, serene blue eyes have calmed my soul on many hard days, but your deep regard for mankind, your political insight, and your sense of humor are some of my favorite things in life! You are so strong in every way, and I can't wait to watch you be the man that God is forming to do great things in this world! I love our completely irreverent sense of humor together, our silly songs we sing that only we could understand, and laughing and loving life with you!

Samuel, our belly laugh! You teach the world every day what it is to know things mere humans never get to see and know. From the moment we became your forever family, you have made all of us better, and you make the whole world better. You define ability. If everyone could be as amused, wise, funny, loving, and sweet as you, the world would be a better place. You are our little slice of Heaven, and we are so thankful for you!

Bo. I think it is funny that God saved you for last because in so many ways in your life, you will always be first. You were born incredaBO, capaBO, and oh so very loveaBO! I enjoy you every day! You are the most like me in political passion, love for animals and adventure, and we even look the most alike! I feel like the most blessed person every day I wake up and I get to be your mama. I always think you are the one who shows me how I could have been, had my life been a little less painful as a child. I love watching you completely devour life! Never stop, my little love!

To our amazing 45th President of the United States of America, President Trump, and the whole beautiful Trump family...how do I thank you all for your bravery, inspiration, your love and support of my work and my family, and the fact that in my opinion, you have saved our beloved America from total destruction? I know history will tell the truth about you, even if the media won't now. In the meantime, I will tell it fearlessly, because you deserve it! Never before have I been more sure of a political decision I made. Every day, I am more amazed at how loyal, loving, and life giving you are as our First Family. You have become friends that have changed me and my entire outlook on the future of this country, and our world! #MAGA, #KAG2020, and beyond!

And my loyal Gippy, who sat protectively next to me through every single word written in this book, you're the best Frenchie in the world and I love you and your little tiger bacon pj's! Grrrr!

Most of all, I thank Jesus Christ, Yeshua, the ONE true God, my personal Lord and Savior, from Whom all good things come, and without Whom, I have only hell and death. Your grace is always sufficient, and your "still small voice" is all the wisdom I have ever known. I walk in your mercy each day, realizing with every breath how undeniable You are, in all the ways you promised you would be, and how lost and fallen and dark I am without You. You are my all, and it is well with my soul! All to your glory and honor, always and forever and ever!

NOTE from the author: Sometimes names, sequence, times, places, and events have been changed or omitted to protect the people who have already endured too many fake news attacks, or simply because I deemed it better to do so for reasons I will write in my tell-all one day :).

NOTES

Chapter 1: Driving His Opponents Mad: Trump's Greatest Accomplishment

1. Washington Post Staff, "Full text: Donald Trump announces presidential bid," *Washington Post*, June 16, 2015, https://www.washingtonpost.com/news/post-politics/wp/2015/06/16/full-text-donald-trump-announces-a-presidential-bid/?utm_term=.e78c74727338.

2. Paul Bedard, "Year One List: 81 major Trump achievements, 11 Obama legacy items repealed," *Washington Examiner*, December 21, 2017, https://www.washingtonexaminer.com/year-one-list-81-major-trump-achievements-11-obama-legacy-items-repealed.

Chapter Two: Mad Skills: How Trump Uses Social Media to Mobilize a Revolution

1. William J. Federer, *Who Is the King in America? And Who Are the Counselors to the King: An Overview of 6,000 Years of History & Why America is Unique* (Amerisearch, Inc.: 2017).

2. C. S. Lewis, *Mere Christianity* (1st HarperCollins ed. San Francisco: HarperSanFrancisco, 2001).

Chapter Three: Triumph Born of Tragedy: What Happened Along the Way

1. Ed Stetzer, "Rick Warren Interview on Muslims, Evangelism & Missions (Responding to Recent News Reports)," *Christianity Today*, March 2, 2012, https://www.christianitytoday.com/edstetzer/2012/march/rick-warren-interview-on-muslims-evangelism-missions.html.

Chapter Four: A Deep Dive into Crazy: My Journey Through the Insanity That Sparked the New Era of Politics

1. Saul D. Alinsky, *Rules for Radicals* (Random House: 1971).

2.   John Mackey, "The Whole Foods Alternative to ObamaCare: Eight things we can do to improve health care without adding to the deficit," *Wall Street Journal*, August 11, 2009, https://www.wsj.com/articles/SB10001424052970204251404574342170072865070.

Chapter Five: The Politics of Anger: How the Left Attacks the Messenger and Blames the Victim

1.   George Orwell, "Politics and the English Language," 1946, http://www.orwell.ru/library/essays/politics/english/e_polit (accessed on July 10, 2018).

2.   Addison Whithecombe, ed. Sky Marsen, quoted in *Communication Studies*, ed. Sky Marsen (New York: Macmillan International Higher Education, 2006), 1, https://books.google.com/books?id=5AAQCwAAQBAJ&pg=PA1&lpg=PA1&dq=When+you+resort+to+attacking+the+messenger+and+not+the+message,+you+have+lost+the+debate.&source=bl&ots=DJIEkMVgo0&sig=eV2RBfEcldil2aya0NtNipauUKg&hl=en&sa=X&ved=0ahUKEwjuhKS22oDcAhVRtlkKHW3jAqUQ6AEIVDAG#v=onepage&q=When%20you%20resort%20to%20attacking%20the%20messenger%20and%20not%20the%20message%2C%20you%20have%20lost%20the%20debate.&f=false.

3.   Robert Heinlein, "The Libertarian in the Lifeboat," http://www.friesian.com/heinlein.htm.

4.   Monica Burke, "New Report Shows Planned Parenthood Raked in $1.5 Billion in Taxpayer Funds Over 3 Years," March 12, 2018, *The Heritage Foundation*, https://www.heritage.org/marriage-and-family/commentary/new-report-shows-planned-parenthood-raked-15-billion-taxpayer-funds.

5.   Susan W. Enouen, "Investigation: Planned Parenthood speeds targeting of minorities," *Life Issues Institute*, February 14, 2017, https://www.lifeissues.org/2017/02/investigation-planned-parenthood-speeds-targeting-minorities.

6. OpenSecrets.org, Center for Responsive Politics, Contributions to Federal Candidates, 2016, https://www.opensecrets.org/pacs/pacgot.php?cmte=C00314617&cycle (accessed on July 10, 2018).=2016.

7. Karl Marx, *The Eighteenth Brumaire of Louis Napoleon* (International Publishers Co.: 1994).

8. Noam Chomsky, *The Common Good* (Odonian Press: 1998).

9. Schuman, Tomas, *Love Letter to America* (Maxims Books: 1984).

Chapter Six: War on the Heartland: How the Left Attacks the Messenger and Blames the Victim

1. Steven D. Price, *1001 Greatest Things Ever Said About California* (Lyons Press: 2007).

2. Ibid.

3. Wayne Hall, "What has research over the past two decades revealed about the adverse health effects of recreational cannabis use?" *Through the Maze: Cannabis and Health International Drug Policy Symposium,* http://onlinelibrary.wiley.com/doi/10.1111/add.12703/full.

4. "Smoking One Joint is Equivalent to 20 Cigarettes, Study Says," *Fox News,* January 29, 2008, http://www.foxnews.com/story/2008/01/29/smoking-one-joint-is-equivalent-to-20-cigarettes-study-says.html.

5. Shaunacy Ferro, "Science Confirms The Obvious: Smoking Pot Makes You Less Motivated," *Popular Science,* July 1, 2013, https://www.popsci.com/science/article/2013-07/science-confirms-obvious-smoking-lot-pot-makes-you-less-motivated.

6. Patrick McGreevy, "Billionaire activists like Sean Parker and George Soros are fueling the campaign to legalize pot," *Los Angeles Times,* November 2, 2016, http://www.latimes.com/politics/la-pol-ca-proposition64-cash-snap-20161102-story.html.

Chapter Seven: Fighting For Your Life: How the Left Embraces Death

1.   CWALAC Staff, "The Negro Project: Margaret Sanger's Eugenic Plan for Black Americans," *Concerned Women For America Legislative Action Committee*, May 1, 2001, https://concernedwomen.org/the-negro-project-margaret-sangers-eugenic-plan-for-black-americans.

2.   Danny David, "Study: Abortion is the leading cause of death in America," *Live Action*, August 11, 2016, https://www.liveaction.org/news/unc-study-demonstrates-effect-of-abortion-on-minorities-and-public-health.

3.   Donald Trump, "My vision for a culture of life," *Washington Examiner*, January 23, 2016, https://www.washingtonexaminer.com/donald-trump-op-ed-my-vision-for-a-culture-of-life.

4.   Tori DeAngelis, "Understanding Terrorism," Monitor on Psychology, 40, no. 10 (November 2009): 60; http://www.apa.org/monitor/2009/11/terrorism.aspx.

5.   DeAngelis, "Understanding Terrorism."

6.   Fathali M. Moghaddam, *How Globalization Spurs Terrorism: The Lopsided Benefits of 'One World' and Why that Fuels Violence* (Westport, Conn.: Praeger, 2008).

7.   Sarah Kershaw, "The Terrorist Mind," *New York Times*, January 9, 2010; http://www.nytimes.com/2010/01/10/weekinreview/10kershaw.html.

8.   Ibid.

9.   Ibid.

10.   Nicolai Sennels, "Psychology: Why Islam Creates Monsters," *Jihad Watch*, September 27, 2013, https://www.jihadwatch.org/2013/09/nicolai-sennels-psychology-why-islam-creates-monsters.

11.   Rusty, "Retired Army Lieutenant Colonel: You Deal with Terrorists by Leaving behind Their 'Crying Widows,' *Political*

Insider, January 12, 2015, https://thepoliticalinsider.com/retired-
army-lieutenant-colonel-you-deal-with-terrorists-by-leaving-behind-
their-crying-widows/#ixzz3OeGciEfW.

12. Matthew Balan, "NYT's Cohen: Islamic Terror Won't Be Solved
     Until Moderates Speak Out," *NewsBusters*, January 12, 2015,
     https://www.newsbusters.org/blogs/matthew-balan/2015/01/12/
     nyts-cohen-islamic-terror-wont-be-solved-until-moderates-speak-
     out#sthash.jxjQhYrE.dpuf.

13. Kershaw, "The Terrorist Mind."

Chapter Eight: Clickbait Voters: How the Media Inflames Division, and How We Let Them Do It

1.   Adolf Hitler, *Mein Kampf*, trans. Ralph Manheim (Houghton
     Mifflin Company: 1998).

2.   Dana Loesch, "Debunking The 14 Biggest Gun Control Lies," *The
     Dana Show*, January 29, 2013, http://danaloeschradio.com/
     debunking-the-14-biggest-gun-control-lies.

3.   "The Truth About 'The Florida Model,'" *Women Against Gun
     Control*, 2012, http://www.wagc.com/ccw-stats.

4.   Vets for Trump, accessed July 10, 2018, https://vets-for-trump.
     com/03/interesting-email-worlds-successful-hate-group.

5.   Maggie Haberman and Amy Chozick, "Hillary Clinton Chose to
     Shield a Top Adviser Accused of Harassment in 2008," *New York
     Times*, January 26, 2018, https://www.nytimes.com/2018/01/26/
     us/politics/hillary-clinton-chose-to-shield-a-top-adviser-accused-of-
     harassment-in-2008.html.

6.   "Political Polarization in the American Public: How Increasing
     Ideological Uniformity and Partisan Antipathy Affect Politics,
     Compromise and Everyday Life," *Pew Research Center*, June 12,
     2014, http://www.people-press.org/2014/06/12/political-
     polarization-in-the-american-public.

Chapter Nine: They May Want Us Crazy: Follow the Money to Madness

1. Shankar Vedantam, "Drug Ads Hyping Anxiety Make Some Uneasy," *The Washington Post*, July 16, 2001, https://www. washingtonpost.com/archive/politics/2001/07/16/drug-ads-hyping- anxiety-make-some-uneasy/8fe2eea2-b780-48cd-9872- 1d3802e83147/?utm_term=.c6da45576389.

2. Cory Franklin, "America's epidemic of over-prescribing," *The Guardian*, June 20, 2011, https://www.theguardian.com/ commentisfree/cifamerica/2011/jun/20/healthcare-drugspolicy.

3. Huxley, Aldous, *Brave New World* (New York: Harper Brothers, 1932).

4. Alan Schwarz, "Idea of New Attention Disorder Spurs Research, and Debate," *New York Times*, April 11, 2014, https://www. nytimes.com/2014/04/12/health/idea-of-new-attention-disorder- spurs-research-and-debate.html.

5. Kessler RC et al., "Prevalence, severity, and comorbidity of 12-month DSM-IV disorders in the National Comorbidity Survey Replication," Arch Gen Psychiatry 62, June 2005: https://www. ncbi.nlm.nih.gov/pubmed/15939839.

6. Jonathan Metzl, "Let's talk about guns, but stop stereotyping the mentally ill," *MSNBC*, April 24, 2013, http://www.msnbc.com/ melissa-harris-perry/lets-talk-about-guns-stop-stereotyping.

7. "The DSM—Psychiatry's Billing Bible," CCHR International: The Mental Health Watchdog, accessed July 6, 2018, https://www. cchrint.org/issues/dsm-billing-bible.

8. Mojtabai R. et al., "Proportion of antidepressants prescribed without a psychiatric diagnosis is growing." Health Aff (Millwood) 30, August 2011: https://www.ncbi.nlm.nih.gov/ pubmed/21821561.

9. "The DSM—Psychiatry's Billing Bible," CCHR International: The Mental Health Watchdog, accessed July 6, 2018, https://www. cchrint.org/issues/dsm-billing-bible.

10. Ibid.

11. Allen J. Frances, M.D., "Female Sexual Dysfunction and Disease Mongering: A twelfth DSM-5 mistake," *PsychologyToday*, March 4, 2013, https://www.psychologytoday.com/us/blog/dsm5-in-distress.

12. Gina Loudon, "American Psychiatric Association: Half of Americans 'Mentally Ill,'" *WND*, June 4, 2013, http://www.wnd.com/2013/06/american-psychiatric-association-half-of-americans-mentally-ill.

13. Ibid.

14. Ian Sample, "New US manual for diagnosing mental disorders published," *The Guardian*, May 18, 2013, https://www.theguardian.com/society/2013/may/18/dsm-5-us-manual-mental-disorders.

15. "Shrinks for Sale: Psychiatry's Conflicted Alliance," CCHR International: The Mental Health Watchdog, accessed July 6, 2018, https://www.cchrint.org/issues/the-corrupt-alliance-of-the-psychiatric-pharmaceutical-industry.

16. Gardiner Harris, "Psychiatrists Top List in Drug Maker Gifts," *New York Times,* June 27, 2007, https://www.nytimes.com/2007/06/27/health/psychology/27doctors.html.

Chapter Ten: Crazy Like a Fox: The Making of the Most Extraordinary President in History

1.   Bandy Lee et al., *The Dangerous Case of Donald Trump: 27 Psychiatrists and Mental Health Experts Assess a President* (New York: Thomas Dunne Books, 2017).

2.   Robert V. V. Hurst, *Life's Fingerprint: How Birth Order Affects Your Path Through Life* (Mandeville, LA: PBO Publishing, 2009).

Chapter Eleven: The Path Back to Sanity: How to Stay Sane When Even the Experts Want You Crazy

1.   "Doing Good Is Good For 2013 Health and Volunteering Study," UnitedHealth Group, accessed July 6, 2018, http://www. unitedhealthgroup.com/~/media/UHG/PDF/2013/UNH-Health-Volunteering-Study.ashx.

2.   Caleb Parke, "Americans who practice yoga contribute to white supremacy, Michigan State University professor claims," *Fox News*, January 29, 2018, http://www.foxnews.com/us/2018/01/29/ americans-who-practice-yoga-contribute-to-white-supremacy-michigan-state-university-professor-claims.html.

3.   Amanda Devlin, "HALF-BAKED: Is going vegan making you STUPID? Ditching dairy could see you drop 13 IQ points, experts warn," *The Sun*, January 23, 2018, https://www.thesun.co.uk/ news/5405801/veganuary-ditching-dairy-iodine-deficiency-drop-13-iq-points.

4.   Henriette van Praag, Monika Fleshner, Michael W. Schwartz, and Mark P. Mattson, "Exercise, Energy Intake, Glucose Homeostasis, and the Brain," Journal of Neuroscience 12 (November 2014): http://www.jneurosci.org/content/34/46/15139.

Chapter Twelve: The Path Back to Sanity: How to Stay Sane When Even the Experts Want You Crazy

1.   Elizabeth Stone, *A Boy I Once Knew* (Algonquin Books: 2002).